You Can Be Set Free!

by William Bumphus

ISBN # 0-89228-086-7

Printed in the
United States of America

INTRODUCTION

William Bumphus is the founder and director of Jesus Inside Prison Ministry, located in Indianapolis, Indiana. Along with his wife Juanita, Rev. Bumphus pastors Faith Center Church International also located in Indianapolis. The Bumphuses have a powerful anointed ability from God to minister life. They have helped ex-convicts become respectable, law-abiding citizens.

This godly couple has helped the poor, even those on welfare, to receive the Gospel so they can change their lifestyle and hold down jobs. They also teach ex-convicts how to break the curse of poverty over their lives and live victoriously for Jesus Christ. The Bumphuses have traveled to prisons throughout the United States and Lagos, Nigeria preaching the Gospel of Jesus Christ. They are truly anointed of God to boldly go where many would not. Yet they go joyously, and the Lord confirms His Word with signs, wonders, and miracles.

ACKNOWLEDGEMENTS

I'd like to first of all thank Jesus for saving me and giving me a life. I'd like to thank my wife Juanita, for her steadfastness and her prayers. Myra Oldham for her expertise in putting these writings together and her support over the years. All my many partners who support this ministry regularly, too many to count, however, I would like to mention a few.

Jim Marshall who has been a supporter and friend of this ministry since day one. Tim Donner and the William H. Donner Foundation. Boonie and Deane Sanders, Ken and Laura Gabel, Lee Grady, Clark Kellogg and the many prisoners who pray and support us. I also want to thank all the Churches that continue to be used of God in helping JIPM.

Thanks!!!

"For God is not unrighteous to forget your work and labor of love, which ye have shewed towards His name, in that ye have ministered to the saints, and do minister." Hebrews 6:10

William Bumphus

Prison Evangelist

YOU CAN HAVE A MIRACLE

Jesus Christ was and is a man/God who specialized in doing miracles for all those who would believe. The recipients were not especially endowed people, but rather common folk with common everyday problems. The very first miracle Jesus performed for someone is recorded in Mark 1:23, "AND THERE WAS IN THEIR SYNAGOGUE A MAN WITH AN UNCLEAN SPIRIT, AND HE CRIED OUT SAYING 'LET US ALONE. WHAT HAVE WE TO DO WITH THEE, THOU JESUS OF NAZARETH? I KNOW WHO THOU ART, THE HOLY ONE OF GOD.' AND JESUS REBUKED HIM, SAYING, 'HOLD THY PEACE AND COME OUT OF HIM.'"

I want you to notice that the Bible says, "THERE WAS A MAN," v.23. Next in verse 30, we see Peter's mother-in-law sick of a fever, and when Jesus is told, He responds by going in and healing her, "AND HE CAME AND TOOK HER BY THE HAND AND LIFTED HER UP: AND IMMEDIATELY, THE FEVER LEFT HER. AND SHE MINISTERED UNTO THEM."

In verses 33-39, you see Jesus healing and setting common people free. In Mark 16:17-20, Jesus said these words to his disciples: "AND THESE SIGNS SHALL FOLLOW THEM THAT BELIEVE: IN MY NAME SHALL THEY CAST OUT DEVILS; THEY SHALL TAKE UP SERPENTS; AND IF THEY DRINK ANY DEADLY THING IT SHALL NOT HURT THEM; THEY SHALL LAY HANDS ON THE SICK, AND THEY SHALL RECOVER. SO THEN AFTER THE LORD HAD SPOKEN UNTO THEM, HE WAS RECEIVED UP INTO HEAVEN AND SAT ON THE RIGHT HAND OF GOD. AND THEY WENT FORTH AND PREACHED EVERYWHERE, THE LORD WORKING WITH THEM AND CONFIRMING THE WORD WITH SIGNS FOLLOWING."

Peter is the first everyday person to believe Jesus and then prove it, by acting on His Word. In Acts 3:1-11, the miracle is recorded for us by Luke. Notice again that the person healed was not somebody special. He was just simply someone in need of a miracle. Because of Peter's insistence on "doing the Word" he was imprisoned (Acts 17). He didn't blame God for his circumstance, instead, he rested in God, he cast all of his cares upon him, because he knew that Jesus cared for him. (1 Peter 5:7)

As a result of his utter dependence upon Jesus and his commitment to the Word of God, an angel came and opened the prison for him, thus providing a way out through a Miracle. Utter dependence and commitment will always cause the Word of God to operate in your life. We call the manifestation of God's Word in our life a Miracle. Throughout the Bible, Jesus and the disciples are noted for the miracles that took place in their ministries. When the people looked upon them as representatives of God, miracles flowed. When we, as people of God, reverence the callings and gifts God places upon those He has called, we also will see and experience more of His miracle working power in our lives.

Somehow, we've allowed the world to replace the Word of God, when it comes to the respect that is due those who labor in the Word. God said to give them double honor. (1 Timothy 5:17)

No miracle is apart from the Word of God. Miracles are for everyone. Occasionally, God in His infinite wisdom will just do something for someone without them even being a believer. However, God's heart and His will is to bless His people. But He can only bless us as far as we will permit Him to. His criterion/His guidelines are His Word and our obedience to it. If we are totally dependent upon Him and His Word, we'll receive miracles. **"IF YE ABIDE IN ME AND MY WORDS ABIDE IN YOU, YE SHALL ASK WHAT YE WILL AND IT SHALL BE DONE UNTO YOU"** (John 15:7).

Doing the Word or acting on faith does not mean that we are to simply quote, or confess our favorite Scriptures, but rather, it means doing the whole Word. We can't confess, "MY GOD SUPPLIES ALL MY NEEDS" (Philippians 4:19)

2

and not give tithes and offerings, and expect for God to supply our needs. They will not get supplied because we're not doing all of the Word. We can't expect Mark 11:23-24 to work in our lives when we totally neglect Mark 11:25.

God has placed ministry gifts in the body to perfect us, for the work of the ministry, for the building up of the Body of Christ. (Ephesians 4:12) But if we don't receive them as the Word has said, but rather criticize and operate in the gift of suspicion, then we will not be perfected or built up, and we will do no work in the kingdom. I know God wants to manifest His glory even more in our personal lives and in our churches, but He's hindered somewhat by our lack of total commitment to the Word of God in these very sensitive areas.

Jesus is looking for those who will worship Him in Spirit and in truth. (John. 4:24) In John 6:63, Jesus said, **"IT IS THE SPIRIT THAT QUICKENETH; THE FLESH PROFITETH NOTHING; THE WORDS THAT I SPEAK UNTO YOU, THEY ARE SPIRIT AND THEY ARE LIFE."**

In John 17:17, Jesus prayed, **"SANCTIFY (separate) THEM THROUGH THY TRUTH; THY WORD IS TRUTH."**

You'll notice that Jesus said his Word is SPIRIT and LIFE and the Word is TRUTH. In order to worship God in Spirit and in truth, we must study, read, meditate, and act out the Word. James says be "DOERS OF THE WORD."

Our lives must reflect the Word; the Bible, and by doing so, we can be assured that our worship is pure. Miracles come when we worship God. As we worship God according to His Word, according to His plan, then Jesus moves among us to meet our deepest and greatest needs. Jesus loves us and His greatest desire is to bless us:

"KNOW YE THAT THE LORD, HE IS GOD. IT IS HE THAT HATH MADE US AND NOT WE OURSELVES: WE ARE HIS PEOPLE AND THE SHEEP OF HIS PASTURE" (Psalm 100).

Jesus stood in the synagogue on a Sabbath day and proclaimed, **"THE SPIRIT OF THE LORD IS UPON ME,**

BECAUSE HE HATH:
1. **ANOINTED ME TO PREACH THE GOSPEL TO THE POOR,**
2. **HE HATH SENT ME TO HEAL THE BROKEN-HEARTED,**
3. **TO PREACH DELIVERANCE TO THE CAPTIVES,**
4. **AND RECOVERING OF SIGHT TO THE BLIND,**
5. **TO SET AT LIBERTY THEM THAT ARE BRUISED,**
6. **TO PREACH THE ACCEPTABLE YEAR OF THE LORD"** (Luke 4:18-19).

The previous six points cover every segment of society. No one is exempt. This also includes prisoners and victims. The captives, I believe, refer to prisoners of all kinds, and them that are bruised – the victims of the world.

Notice that it is the same Jesus, the same Word of God for all people. Victims of crimes, as well as the perpetrators of crimes, need the same Jesus, and He is available. The Bible says, **"ALL HAVE SINNED AND COME SHORT OF THE GLORY OF GOD"** (Romans 3:23).

1 John 5:17 says "ALL UNRIGHTEOUSNESS IS SIN."

Regardless of what our reasons are, we shall be held accountable for all sin." Notice Galatians 5:19-21 and Revelation 21:8.

Notice also the list of sins that will matter to God. He lists liars, along with the murderers, as going to the lake of fire.

Someone might argue when defending a victim, that they have a right to hate, or when defending a prisoner, that they had a right to do what they did because of thus and so. However, the Word of God is quite clear. SIN is SIN. Unforgiveness is unforgiveness, and repentance is the only way into the presence of God.

Rich or poor, free person, victim or prisoner, we all must abide by the rules of God's kingdom, if we are to have any kind of peace. Everyone must label sin as sin and then get rid of unforgiveness and sin through repentance, thus making room for God to move on your behalf as you adhere to

His Word. In Jeremiah 1:12, God says, "I WILL HASTEN MY WORD TO PERFORM IT." God will make sure that everything He has said in His Word will come to pass. So, if you want justice, act on God's Word. If you want mercy, act on GOD'S WORD.

The greatest miracle I've experienced was when I totally began to rely on Jesus and committed myself to the Word of God. If at this point in your life, you will totally begin to rely upon Jesus, you can have a miracle. Let me share with you the miracle power of God to change lives.

THE EARLY YEARS

As I begin telling my story, I am continually awed by the miracle-working power of Jesus Christ. I am also extremely grateful for His grace. I was born on December 14, 1946, to Mosella and William Bumphus. Mama was sixteen and so was my father. He lied about his age so he could get in the military. We lived with my mother's mother, Mrs. Tallie Perry. My grandmother went to a nice Christian Methodist Episcopal (C.M.E.) Church, a facade strictly for status.

My grandmother was not with her husband, and was a regular gin drinker. My grandmother felt it was disgraceful for her teenage daughter (my mother) to have a baby. My grandmother hated my father, and that is why she disliked me, so she tried to keep things quiet about their marriage. I was told that a few weeks after I was born, my grandmother put me in the warm morning stove with intentions of burning me up. I was delivered from being burned alive by my father who happened to be home on leave. My mother moved out shortly after this incident, and my father went back to the service.

Mama was not saved and was doing the things that the

sinful nature dictates. Mama, her Mother and brother all drank. Months later my mother became pregnant with my sister Karen by my father. Shortly afterwards, she met another man and left my father for him. My father was always involved in gambling and other criminal activities. When he got out of the service, he continued in these activities. Although I didn't know it at the time, it would be twelve years before I would come to know my father. I was raised on the west side of Indianapolis and the inner-city area where I lived was heavily impoverished. This area was not unlike the poor section in most cities in the United States at that time. The house I lived in was located in the Twelfth Street alley. My earliest recollections are of dire poverty. A typical memory includes waking up in the morning, Mama gone, no food in the house, and my brothers and sisters hollering and crying for something to eat. We never had enough to eat it seemed. Often we went to bed hungry and sometimes cold.

Out of desperation I began to canvas the neighborhood for food. I remember raiding people's gardens, because I was so hungry. One morning I noticed a doughnut truck delivery man placing several boxes of doughnuts on the steps of the neighborhood grocery store. I investigated, and sure enough the doughnuts were fresh. I didn't take all of them, because I didn't want to get caught. This kind of pilfering went on for a time, until I got so bold that I began to go into the grocery store and steal.

Where we lived, everyone was in the same shape. Drinking, fighting, and just barely making it from day to day was the normal way of life. This was a very traumatic time for everyone in the neighborhood because of the dire living conditions. For example, I remember one day we were all playing outside, and my sister Mary was sitting on the back of a car. A man got in the car, not knowing that Mary was sitting on it, and just took off with a roar. Mary slipped off the trunk but was able to hold on to the bumper. With the forward jerk of the car, Mary was caught underneath the car and dragged. She couldn't let go of the bumper because her ear had somehow gotten hooked in between the metal bumper and the car.

Everyone was shouting and hollering trying to get the man's attention so he would stop the car, but he was still unaware that Mary was hanging onto the bumper. I took off running so fast after the car that I ran out of my shoes. I finally caught the car, and got the driver's attention. He was drunk. Mary was rushed to the hospital in an ambulance, with her ear just hanging on by a little piece of skin. The side of her face was raw from being dragged like that. Fortunately, the people at the hospital sewed and bandaged her up really good.

I also remember one time when our house caught on fire. I was asleep when it broke out, and everyone thought I had escaped from the burning house. My mother just happened to come home and found out that all the other kids were out of the house, but I was still inside. She ran in and carried me out. Many years later, I came to understand that God had spared my life. I was the last one rescued from that fire!

I talk with Christians all the time who really don't know what a curse poverty is. Anyone who has ever lived in poverty knows beyond a shadow of a doubt just how bad the curse of poverty really is. I didn't know it at the time, but the Bible even calls poverty a curse (Deut. 28:15-68). This curse was really having an effect on my family, especially on me.

For example, when I was ten, I woke up one morning and went down the stairs where we lived and noticed the alley literally filled with cartons of cigarettes. I began to gather them up and take them upstairs. My mother was not at home, so I began to practice smoking. When my mother came home, I informed her of my great find, and she was very happy. This meant she could make some money selling those cigarettes. She kept some for herself and gave me permission to smoke, so I kept some too.

Before I go any further, I want you to know that I loved my mother more than anything. She did the best she could with what she had to work with. She accepted Jesus Christ as her personal Savior before she went on to be with the Lord, on May 30, 1988.

At the age of twelve, I met my father for the first time. We had moved again (it seemed we moved every other month), and we were now living on Missouri Street in the rear alley. My father drove into our poverty-stricken area in a beautiful, shining, new, convertible car, and three women were with him. My mother introduced me to him, and my dad took me with him out to the car to show me off to his women friends. I had not received much attention before this time that I can remember. I believe the attention I received from him and these women made a marked impression on me.

From this time until I received Jesus Christ, my father was my idol, and I wanted to be like him. I always sought his approval. Later, I moved in with him and loved the new lifestyle I was experiencing. Everything seemed to be going well at this time. But, my father was in the street world, which meant that he never had a job but made his living by gambling, pimping, and stealing. However, he had a great respect for education, and encouraged me to get an education, so I began really enjoying school. I saw education as a means to help my mother. However, the devil had other plans for me.

SATAN HAS HIS PLANS TOO

When I was fourteen, I was playing with some of my friends, and we were throwing rocks at each other. We ran through the neighborhood onto the roofs of old houses, and we began flying roofing shingles at each other like Frisbees.

8

All of sudden, a shingle struck me in the eye. I was rushed to the hospital and over a period of several months I had two eye operations. After the operations, I was left blind in my left eye. While I was in the hospital, the doctors wanted to remove my left eye without my knowledge, and my father had given his consent. My mother came to the hospital to inform me of their plans. She said, "If you don't want the operation, we will leave this hospital right now."

So we both then left, and I moved back in with her. I had only lived with my father a few months, but already his lifestyle had adversely affected me. He was trying to get custody of me, but by then my fascination with my father was deteriorating,

TRAGEDY STRIKES AGAIN

My mother and I and my brothers and sisters had a nice summer, but as winter was coming around, tragedy struck again. We lived in a duplex, and on the other side of the duplex lived some men who made their living selling junk. One day my mother noticed that these men were burning old car batteries and selling the lead.

It was really cold, and we were out of coal, so she asked the men for some of the batteries to burn in the warm morning stove. A week later, we noticed that my five-year-old sister and six-year-old brother were constantly throwing up and not able to eat. My mother rushed them to the hospital only to find out that they had lead poisoning. The whole family, which at that time included three other sisters and one brother, were also affected. We all had to be hospitalized. My younger brother and sister died as a result of that lead poisoning.

Their deaths were very devastating to the whole family, and it caused my mother to begin to change. She found a job and slowed down considerably in her drinking. She never went out partying from that time until she went home to be with Jesus. I changed too.

We didn't have insurance, so the state buried the kids, I felt ashamed of our poverty, so I took it out on everyone outside my neighborhood who wasn't poor like we were. For example, I joined the neighborhood gang, and I went around beating up people, stealing, and getting drunk. At fifteen I dropped out of school and began staying out all night. I stole everything, especially cars. At the age of sixteen, I was arrested for the first time for V.T. (Vehicle-Taking) and was given six months probation and fined $115.

At the age of seventeen, I was locked up for the first time. I was sentenced to serve 180 days (6 months) at the Indiana State Farm and was sent to the county jail to await transport to the Indiana State Farm. I was so scared, but I knew that I had better not show any signs of fear. I'd heard tales of rape and violence in prison, especially toward young men. I thought that if I just stayed to myself, no one would bother me. I was definitely wrong. In fact, when you stay to yourself, it makes the other inmates around you think you are afraid for sure.

I was approaching my eighteenth birthday, and here I was, locked up in prison! Just a few days before my eighteenth birthday, an older inmate began threatening me, telling me what he was going to do to me. However, an escape in another cell block caused the jailer to put the whole jail on restriction. This meant we were kept in our cells the whole time except for two hours per day for showers and recreation. This went on for a month.

During this time that older inmate kept hollering down the hallway from his cell to mine about how he was going to make me his girlfriend. And, of course, I hollered back telling him what I was going to do to him if he tried! This all happened in 1966 at the height of the Civil Rights Movement. This inmate was black; all cell blocks were segregated at that time.

Also, at that time, black Muslims were increasing in numbers as well. An older man shared my cell - he was a Black Muslim from New York. He said he'd been with Malcolm X and had been on the run for some violent acts against the government. Some of his friends had been stopped as they traveled through Indiana with carloads of weapons. This man began to talk to me about my heritage as a black man, about the Black Muslim Movement as it was called then, and how to carry myself in prison. He told me to stop hollering at the inmate who was threatening to make me his girlfriend.

He said, "Just wait for the cell doors to roll back, be the first one out, and hit that inmate with everything you've got - and don't let up! That's the way to take care of that situation!" You can imagine what happened. I was scared, but I was not about to be anybody's girlfriend! As soon as the doors began to roll open, I slid out of mine, and before the inmate knew what was happening, I was in his cell hitting him with everything I had in me. When it was all over, it took all the fight out of him, and all the fear out of me. I learned to always take the first lick, and not to let up until nothing was left in the other person.

I stayed in jail six weeks before I was finally transported to the Indiana State Farm. I was so surprised when I got there, because it seemed like all my partners in crime from my old neighborhood had wound up there! My experiences at the Indiana State Farm only taught me to be a better criminal. I wanted to be a pimp and street hustler, just like my father was at that time.

The only things that interested me were stories the older prisoners told about their crimes. They talked about pimping women, shooting and selling dope, cashing bad checks, and burglarizing. I learned these things well from listening to them.

I was finally released from the Indiana State Farm in April

11

1967. I left much worse than when I entered. Immediately upon my release, I sought out old friends and began putting my criminal plans into action. I began stealing, burglarizing, getting high, drinking, and popping pills. By November 1967, I was locked up again for robbery and burglary. I stayed in the county jail eight months trying to fight the case. Finally, I got a plea agreement for one year at the Indiana State Farm.

During this incarceration, I got more involved in Islam. I studied under Elijah Mohammed and received my X. The X meant that we were rejecting our slavemasters' names we were given when we were brought over from Africa. Thus, my new name, William X, meant that I no longer accepted Bumphus as my last name. I also took it upon myself to change my entire name to one that I thought was Arabic. I began to refer to myself as Hashaii Abdul Hakim. By my own estimation, I became politically conscious.

The autobiography of Malcolm X drastically changed my life. In fact, many incarcerated Blacks could identify with Malcolm X. He had been in and out of trouble all his life. He'd been converted to Islam in prison and had educated himself and became a great spokesman. I could readily identify with him, because I wanted to be somebody. However, I knew the opportunities to make something of myself just did not exist for me.

I knew if I were ever going to be someone, I had to make something happen myself, so I began to articulate my new-found religion throughout the inmate population. I also began to write poetry and submit them to various newspapers under my so-called Arabic name. My ego began to soar as the material was published. I thought I was a celebrity so I became more vocal.

Of course, this didn't go unnoticed by the prison administration, so harassment by the officials intensified.

At this point, I tried to stage a sit-down on the job. The administration got wind of it and began to confront me. They said they didn't like my haircut, which was an afro,which was popular in those days, and they used harassment about my haircut to accomplish their purpose. I went on and on, saying that my haircut was all right and that there were no rules prohibiting my hairstyle. This resulted in them sending me to the hole.

I served seven days down there in that dark, dirty place, cursing and hollering about how my rights had been violated. Finally, I was removed from there and placed in administrative segregation. Administrative segregation is a place in the prison where you are put in a single cell and kept away from other prisoners for a variety of reasons. It's punishment for breaking the rules. I was in segregation for forty-five days.

My family was informed that I had suffered a nervous breakdown and could not receive visits. My mother accepted the prison officials' explanation and there was little I could do about it.

I remember at this time that a guard passed by my cell and threw me a Bible and told me to read it. However, it is impossible to understand a spiritual book with a natural mind without an instructor or teacher – plus the fact that I was into Islam, which didn't help matters any.

At that time, I believed that the Bible was simply the white man's lie and that slave owners and the Ku Klux Klan had used certain passages from the Bible to justify their treatment of black slaves. I felt they used the Bible so they could make black slaves accept their position in life as coming from God by teaching that blacks were under a curse.

I didn't believe that the Bible was the inspired Word of God, but rather that men wrote it and therefore twisted it for their own purposes. Jesus, I believed, was merely a good, moral man – just a prophet like Mohammed. The only devils were blue-eyed ones, I thought. Man, was I deceived! Satan had me blinded to the truth (2 Cor.4: 4), and I was well on my way to more hell on earth, plus ultimate hell upon my departure from this life.

Even though I was in this pit, as so many are, I was actually searching for truth the only way I knew how. There were even times people tried to share Jesus with me; however, I had my mind made up about Christians. I felt most of them were weak individuals who needed to use Jesus as a crutch. At that time, Islam was a very militant religion. To me, Christianity seemed only to be for the weak.

After my stay in the hole and in segregation, I was released back into the general prison population. I must also relate that I was very serious about what I believed. I felt like I was a part of the solution to the black man's problem and to the case of racial injustice in the world.

At that time, I really thought that the solution to the black man's problems was found in understanding our heritage, culture, and Islam. What I didn't realize was that until a man's heart is changed, he himself can never change – no matter what color he is. And only God can change a man's heart.

And of course, I wanted to be accepted. I wanted people to think well of me, so when several older inmates seemed to think I had something on the ball and wanted to hear what I had to say, this added to my warped sense of self-esteem.

Although some things I was learning about racism and my heritage were true, I was still going about changing things the wrong way. These older brothers were cool in the prison yard and were respected as 'players.' A player is a street name for a person who makes his living from criminal activities. They are pimps, cons, drug dealers, and so forth. So when these older criminals told me I needed to be cooler, I readily listened.

Several days into our discussions, they introduced me to heroin, explaining how this would help me and that everyone was doing it. The drugs were smuggled into the prison in various ways, and they were plentiful.

14

Although this was taboo in Islam, in the same way pork is forbidden , I still indulged. Of course this radically changed my perspective on many things, but I still believed that Islam was the only true religion and definitely the only religion for the black man.

But with this introduction to drugs, I began to use all kinds of drugs until my release some four months later. I would become a heroin addict for the next ten years.

MY PLAN FOR SUCCESS

Upon my release in early 1968, I again began to implement my plan for success. I met a young lady and convinced her that prostitution was the only way to live, so she began to make money by this livelihood.

I became popular in my area and began to enlarge my activities. I gambled more and began to sell slum clothing and jewelry. I was taking pills and drinking for about a month after my release, trying to reach that same high I had known in the joint. One night I was entertaining some friends in my favorite night club, by buying them drinks. We were all dancing and having a good time. But that night, I overdosed on pills and alcohol.

A couple of friends I'd met in prison picked me up and carried me out of the club. They in turn took me on my way to the big time. They taught me how to acquire heroin and we all began to hang out together and also began to make money together. As our habits grew, so did our criminal activities. I was arrested during the next two years for a wide variety of criminal activities, but there was nothing solid enough to hold me for long. As my habit for heroin grew, I had to do more and more things to make more money. I was pimping, robbing, and slumming – anything to get a dollar.

At this time, my friends and I also began to steal and cash checks. One day in early 1970, a friend of mine and I took two checks to our favorite check-cashing place. I had an arrangement with this business owner. I would steal checks of all kinds out of people's mailboxes. I would endorse them and sell them to him for fifty percent of the total of the checks.

But one day, upon arriving at our favorite check-cashing place, we were told by the owner that he couldn't do any more business with us for awhile. He had to lay low because the Postal Inspector had contacted him, and he was afraid that he was being followed and probably even investigated. I felt like he was telling us the truth, because we had been doing business with him for well over eight months and we knew we could trust him. However, I was getting pretty sick and I had to have some money for heroin.

A heroin addict gets deathly sick, if he can't get the drug. The symptoms are terrible, and I needed a fix, so I pressed the issue with him. He cashed a smaller check and said that if I returned later, he'd cash the larger check. I went to get some dope, but there was a panic on. That means that the drug was getting hard to find due to the arrest of drug dealers and confiscation of the drug.

For the money I had, I couldn't get what I needed. I needed a little more money in order to get a fix, so we went back and waited across the street at my mother's house, until the time came for us to meet our contact man.

As we approached the business to get the large check cashed, my partner thought he'd seen a gun on the man that was standing on the corner. However, in our desperate need for drugs, we soon dismissed that. Once inside the building, I placed the check on the counter and signed it. I was about to hand it to the owner, when he informed me that the FBI was observing the whole deal. He also informed me that they had followed him home from the bank and were waiting to talk to me.

As we turned toward the door to leave, we noticed that the gentleman we thought had a gun, indeed was carrying one, and was blocking our escape through the door. Our only course of action was to surrender, which we did readily. Several months later I was convicted of forgery of U.S. checks and sentenced to two years at the Federal Prison in Terre Haute, Indiana.

Upon arriving at the Federal Prison, I began to try to put my life back together again. By then I was beginning to get tired of this prison life. I wanted to stay out of prison; it wasn't fun anymore. I did a lot of thinking and finally thought I had come up with the answer. So far, everyone and everything, including God (I thought), had let me down.

Therefore, I first deduced that there was no God. Secondly, if I was going to amount to anything in life, I had to get off shooting dope, and I had to at least get a high-school education. So I abandoned my enthusiasm for Islam, even though I still felt the same way about Jesus, the Bible, and the white man. In prison, I enrolled in school to pursue a GED, and I vowed never to shoot dope again. However, in prison, I met some inmates that turned me on to some LSD, so I began to trip on acid. The best intentions of man are not enough to change his life; it takes a power much greater than man – it takes God Himself!

I also kept up my writing, and it was still being published from time to time. Things seemed to be going along just fine for the first eight months of my "new life," and then tragedy struck again. My grandmother on my father's side died of cancer. At that time I'd grown closer to my grandmother than to any other member of the family. She always tried to help me out a little, and I felt saddened by her death. My father arranged for me to have a twenty-four-hour leave from prison so I could attend her funeral.

Upon my arrival home, my family and friends were glad and waiting to see me. Of course we began to drink and

17

smoke dope. It wasn't long before we were all drunk, and as was our custom, we began arguing and fighting among each other.

Well, as things would have it, I woke up the next morning in the local jail, face swollen and teeth missing. We had all begun to fight, moved outside with our ruckus, where I slipped and knocked myself out when I fell in the street. However, it would be months before I realized the truth, because that night was a total blackout to me.

I was sent back to the prison days later and placed in the hole for what they termed, "breach of promise." Of course, sitting in a stripped cell, with pain running up and down your face, realizing that you don't know how you got in that state – all of that can have a very negative effect upon an already negative person. After three days in the hole, I was taken to stand before the disciplinary board. They informed me that I could have some of my good days taken away from me for this incident.

Most prisons have a reward system for good behavior. In Indiana back then, a prisoner can earn a day for a day. In other words, if you receive a five years sentence, and you don't get into any trouble, you can earn a day of good time for every day you serve. Therefore, you could serve only two years and six months for a five-year sentence.

But the prison officials didn't believe that I was innocent. I was released from the hole and placed in another unit.

As I contemplated on these recent events, I became more hostile. I was feeling very sorry for myself, I was hurt, and it seemed as though no one cared whether I lived or died. The fact that I was in a terrible unit didn't help anything. I'd only been in this unit a day and already the noise was getting to me; it was unbearable. You see, I had come from a single cell that had its own door. Therefore, I had privacy and quietness.

But in this new unit, I was placed in a dormitory with approximately 250 men. Everyone was allowed to have his own radio and tune it to whatever station he wanted. And in another area close by was the television set. So throughout the dorm, men played cards, dominoes, chess, and so forth. The noise coming from everyone doing something all at the same time was unbearable.

The second day when I was in the TV room, I noticed a young white boy coming up the steps into the unit. I overheard a few inmates say he had just been released from the hole. Suddenly about ten inmates came rushing upon him from all sides, grabbed him, took him into the showers, and all of them began to rape him. I noticed that the guard simply turned his head.

To this day, I don't know what that was all about. However, this had a very sickening effect upon me, coupled with everything else. The next day I was assigned to work in the wicker shop where we made baskets and some furniture. As I worked and thought about everything, especially about the fact that they were considering taking away some of the days I'd earned for good behavior, I decided to give them a real reason for taking my good days away from me. I began to smash up all the chairs and everything in the shop.

After I was subdued, I was finally taken to someone in charge. I was sentenced to seven days in a strip cell. A strip cell was located in the detention section of the prison, and it's usually, dark, cold and damp. It has no toilet, simply a hole in the floor that is operated from the outside. There's no sink for washing or for drinking water.

However, I was brought bologna sandwiches and a cup of water three times a day. I was used to this and knew how to occupy my mind. I would sing, shadow box, exercise, and think. Thinking was the hardest part. Finally, I was released after seven days. I was dirty and literally stank from not having taken any showers. I was escorted up to the disciplinary board. Once there I was informed that they were not going to take any of my good days away from me, but they were going to have me serve the remainder of my

19

time in a segregation unit. In other words, I was going to be put in a cell alone away from other prisoners.

I had about four months to go when they put me in segregation. Segregation was better than the hole in that you did have a toilet, a face bowl, a desk, and could come out once a week for showers.

In segregation, there was no contact with other prisoners at all; each of our doors were made of steel with slots through which we received our mail. I began to really appreciate the quietness, and I used my time to read. Fellow inmates had smuggled my black history library to me, so I was doing a lot of this type of studying and writing, enforcing my position of being a victim of this society's racism. I lost track of time.

One day my door was opened, and I was told to come out and get dressed because I was going home. I prepared to leave in total disbelief, but to my pleasant surprise, I was actually going home. My brother, who had just been released from the army, was there to pick me up. It felt good to see family, and it was even better to know I was free.

As we traveled back to Indianapolis, I began to reflect on my life. It was painful. I didn't want to go back to prison ever again.

BACK HOME AGAIN

Mama and the rest of the family were glad to see me and of course they all had good reasons why they were unable to visit or write me. I had made up my mind that I was through shooting heroin into my veins, and I was determined to make it this time without drugs. I had my GED, and I knew it counted for something.

I met a young lady and moved in with her far away from my associates and that drug environment. I looked for employment but was unable to find anything that paid anything because of my past history. So I finally went back to work with the same people my mother was working for.

At the time, my mother worked for a silk screen printing company, which also put up tents. I worked putting up tents and later learned to do silk screen printing. I was living a quiet life, I thought. I would work all week and drink and smoke dope and take a little LSD, just enough, I reasoned to get me through the day.

On the weekends, my girl friend and I would party with pills, alcohol, weed and LSD. I reasoned that this was better than shooting dope. After all, I was working every day and not stealing. This continued for about nine months. I had set a record! I hadn't been locked up for doing anything bad.

One day as I rested at home, someone knocked on the door. It was someone whom I'd known from childhood. After we greeted one another, he told me that he'd gotten strung out on drugs in Vietnam and that he was sick and needed a ride so he could pick up some dope. After assuring me that this would be the first and last time he would ask me, I finally consented to take him to get some dope.

However, several weeks later he knocked on my door again. Well, I knew what this was leading up to, so I told him very adamantly that this was indeed the last time. I drove him to pick up a couple of his friends and then took them to the place where they could get drugs. All of a sudden as I waited for them in my car in the alley, they came running out of the dope house telling me to step on the gas. My first thought was of being arrested, but as we got further down the road, I realized what had taken place.

They'd lied to me; they'd set me up. They had used me and my transportation to rob the dope house. They had only taken drugs, no money, but to make matters worse, that evening I found out that there was a contract out on my life. I returned home with the drugs as part of my payment and a shotgun for helping them. I stayed home from my job hoping for things to cool off. After a week or so, I had to emerge from my home, because I had shot up all those drugs, so I was beginning to feel those morning sicknesses once again – the withdrawal pains from the drugs.

All rational thinking again began to evade me. I deduced that I had only been fooling myself with those thoughts of living a straight life. I knew that my lot in life was to be a dope fiend, so I purposed to be the best one around. I got together with a guy I knew, and we began our crime spree. The young lady I had been staying with also got involved as a prostitute. As we made more money, our habits grew. I continued this for about a year.

One morning as we came together to map out our course of action for that day, we decided to burglarize our fence,the man who bought stolen merchandise. The night before, we had thrown a concrete brick through a downtown stereo shop and had grabbed a bunch of top-quality speakers. We met this gentleman and sold him quite a few of them. He didn't have enough money to buy them all, so he gave us his telephone number and told us to call him in the morning.

We arranged to purchase some drugs, and then we went home. I had saved some drugs for the morning, but my partner was sick and in a hurry to get some money for some drugs the next morning. I called this man who wanted to buy the other speakers, but I got no answer, so we decided to give him a visit. Upon arriving at his house, we knocked on the door, but still there was no answer.

As we peered through the window, we noticed several pieces of merchandise still in their original cartons. The temptation was so great that we went in and began to load our car with this merchandise. As we backed out of the driveway, several police cars pulled in behind us, preventing our escape.

Of course we were arrested on the spot, sent to jail, and given a high bond, so that we couldn't get out of jail. The following day, we were taken out of our cells to go talk with a detective. The detective told us that there had been a series of thefts in the neighborhood where we had been busted, and he felt we might know something about them. We didn't, and we told him that we had no knowledge of that area.

The detective promised us that if we came clean and cleared up these incidents by confessing to them, we would not be charged with these thefts. Plus, he assured us that we would have our bonds lowered so we could make bail. My partner was in agreement with the idea, but I totally refused to plead guilty to something I hadn't done.

Late that night as I lay in a cell where the door didn't lock, an officer approached my cell, and someone yelled, "Put out your flashlight!" The officer demanded, "Who is the smart guy?" and in turn the inmate said, "It's your mama." The officer came directly to my cell door and asked me, "Why did you say that?" I acted like I was asleep. He then said, "I know you're not asleep. If you don't answer me, I'm going to send guards into the cell block to bring you out."

I answered, "I didn't say anything!" Then he accused me, saying, "Are you calling me a liar!" He arranged for me to be pulled out of my unit immediately. The authorities took me into a small holding area, and the detective called for eight large deputies. They filled the holding area I was in and began to threaten my life, saying they would break my nigger back. I knew what this meant; I was being set up for something.

The next day I was called out again. The same detective asked me the same questions again. I realized what was going on and knew I had to get out of there because I had a better chance of survival on the street, plus, my partner had already confessed.

So my partner and I accepted more charges with the understanding that we would never be charged with them. The next morning the front page of the newspaper read, "Major Burglary Ring Busted. Two Men Confess to 33 Burglaries and Thefts." Our bonds were lowered, so I was able to make bond.

I separated from my partner and hired a good attorney. Still, the damage was done, our fate was sealed, and the prosecutor was not offering any deals. In fact, the prosecutor told my attorney he would prosecute me to the fullest extent of the law. Since I was looking at a possible sixty years, I decided to jump bond. I just didn't go back to court. I stayed with friends for about a year.

The following year, the young lady who was still with me found a job that didn't deduct for taxes. This gave us enough money to purchase a place of our own, so we got married. I gambled a little, stole a little, shot a little dope, but mostly I drank. I was paranoid and lived in a constant state of fear. I was tired of doing time and didn't want to go back to prison. After four years of being on the run, I'd finally had enough. I was taking acid heavily, trying to work up courage to get out of my situation.

While at some of my associates' house doing acid and drinking, I began to have a bad trip. I began talking very vulgarly to the hostess, forgetting the fact she was kind enough to let us stay with her. After a few more vulgar remarks, my cousin gave the hostess a 25 automatic pistol and told her to shoot me.

She demanded, "Quit speaking to me in that manner! Respect my house or else I'll blow your brains out." To prove her point, she pointed the gun toward me. I was tripping hard and thought she was, too. So I continued to curse her while daring her to shoot. The next morning I remember waking up in the back seat of a car with a terrible pain in my right knee. She had shot me in the knee. I was fortunate that the bullet went clear through my leg, instead of lodging in my knee. I was too paranoid and afraid to go to the hospital, because I knew that the hospital had to report gunshot wounds.

24

I asked to be taken over to my mother's house so she could nurse my knee. I was filled with rage and anger, and the thought of murdering that woman who'd shot me was constantly on my mind. I tried to drown the thoughts out by drinking, but nothing worked. I wanted to hurt so many people to get even for everything I'd suffered. I had so much hate in my heart, I felt like I was going to explode.

One night as my friends and I were drinking, I determined that I'd had enough of living this way. I was going to get up the next morning, get some dope, stick up a bank, and get out of town. If I got caught, I decided I would not go peaceably. But Someone else had a different plan for my life.

REVENGE THAT BACKFIRED

That night I was with the same young lady and her sister (the woman who shot me). On our way to a friend's house to party, I decided I wanted to get revenge against the woman who'd shot me. I stole her car and was going to rob a bank in the morning using her car.

I parked the car several streets from my mother's house, went into the house, and passed out on the couch. To my dismay, I was awakened by flashing lights and the sound of bullhorns. Before I could get myself together, the authorities were handcuffing me. The young lady and her sister had called the police and told them I was a fugitive. My mother also told the police that the woman had shot me in the knee, so they also began looking for the woman. The outcome was that we were all arrested and taken to jail.

This was Friday night, which meant I would have to stay in jail until Monday to be officially charged. So far, they didn't know who I really was. At the time of arrest, I was using an alias, and had identification to match. I was being charged with drunk and disorderly conduct. However,

I just knew they were going to find out who I really was because they had my fingerprints.

By this time I had been arrested twenty-three times. Eleven of the arrests were for felonies. I had served time in prison three times. As I lay in jail, I wished so much that I could have lived my life all over again and done things differently.

"Where had all the trouble started?" I wondered. I knew I was going to prison for a longer stay this time. I was so tired of doing time. What could I do? No one loved me or cared about me, except maybe my Mama. Life was terrible. I had no answers. I couldn't see any hope in sight. "Who could ever get me out of this terrible fix," I wondered. Little did I know that there was a God in Heaven who loved me more than anyone else on earth had ever loved me. He knew me in all my weaknesses, and loved me in spite of them.

I didn't realize it then, but my heart was reaching out to Him because I needed Someone to save me from the mess I'd made of my life. God was there all the time, just waiting for me to turn to Him.

GOD'S PLAN

On Sunday morning I was awakened by a disturbance in the cell block. A short older white man was outside the cell block talking a bunch of Jesus stuff. A few inmates told him to shut up and take it someplace else. He didn't. His preaching also began to annoy me. But something on the inside of me was trying to reach out to this man and what he was saying. As the preacher concluded, he invited men to come to the front of the cell block and let him pray with them. Pride was telling me, "Stay where you are. You don't need that!" After all, there was really nothing to that Jesus stuff, or so I thought.

I thought, "Jesus was just a good man, but He can't help me now."

But something deep inside me reasoned, "What can it hurt? After all, it's only a prayer." Besides, I knew I needed all the help I could get. So I went down front and allowed this white man to pray for me.

The next morning I went to court and just as I expected, they'd found out my true identity. They knew I had been on the run for four years. I was taken from the courthouse to the Marion County Jail. I was put in a holding cell until a cell block was assigned to me. Amazingly, something had been awakened in me because of that prayer. I heard myself praying, "Jesus, if You are real, put me in a good cell block."

However, I was assigned to the worst cell block in the jail. Because of that, I reasoned, "Jesus isn't alive! He didn't even hear that prayer!" Because I thought that prayer hadn't been answered, I was determined never to get sucked into anything like that Jesus stuff again. I reasoned, "I just responded to that preacher, because I let my emotions get out of control. From now on I will make sure I stay in control of my emotions!"

Little did I know that God was even then moving in my behalf to answer my prayer!

He not only had heard my prayer, but He was busy arranging circumstances so that I would come to Him. He was arranging for my salvation from this horrible life of sin and crime! I would later come to know the wonderful faithfulness of God. The prison officials assigned me to a maximum security cell block located on the fourth floor. By the time I finally entered my cell, I was tired, and all I wanted to do was lie down and rest. After a while a guy came down to find out what I was charged with and tried to hold a conversation with me. I was not in the mood.

Before I could ask him to leave my cell, he said, "Can I ask you a personal question?" I thought to myself, "What's wrong with him, asking me if he can ask me a personal question? Is he a homosexual? Or worse yet, does he think I'm one?" All these questions began to cloud my mind. You don't get too personal in jail, but for some reason unknown to me at the time, I consented and said, "Go ahead. Ask me your question."

So he popped the ultimate question, "Do you know Jesus Christ as your personal Savior?" As you read this, if you are a Christian, you are probably rejoicing right now because of this question. But believe me, I wasn't. I was shaken up.

This was the third time in two days someone tried to share Jesus with me. I wasn't raised in a Christian home, so by now I was getting superstitious.

I reasoned that since this had occurred in such a short period of time, I must be jinxed. That made me think even more that I would get the maximum sentence. So instead of shouting for joy, I became very verbal and ordered that nut out of my room. "What nerve!" I thought. After I rested and ate chow that evening, I decided to explore the cell block. I wanted to see if I knew anyone in there. I remember passing a cell and seeing a strange sight. Five inmates were gathered together in a circle, holding hands praying.

The following day they invited me down to their Bible study. I decided to go. As these inmates began to tell their testimonies about how Jesus came into their lives, I knew that there was something different going on here. I knew this was real. These men talked and acted like they really knew Jesus. Everyone I'd ever heard always communicated a historical Jesus – about a man who had lived and died 2,000 years ago. But these fellows talked about a Jesus who was alive right now.

Not only was Jesus alive, they said, but He wanted to save people and help them. I had heard about the Jesus who had walked the shores of Galilee, healed the sick, and died on the Cross. All I knew about Salvation was it had something to do with death and Heaven and hell. But these guys were talking about a Jesus who cared about you so much that He even cared about how much time you got.

This grabbed my attention. I wanted to hear more. I heard that Jesus died for my sins, cared about everything that concerned me, and would help me with my case. The condition was, that I ask Him to come into my heart to be my Savior. As I reflected on all this, I began to think, "Maybe this Jesus stuff is real. What if Jesus is the Son of God? What if He is more than a prophet? What if there really is a Heaven and a hell? What if there really is life after death?" These thoughts and questions pushed their way into my consciousness, and I had to find some answers. One night, several weeks later while these fellows were praying, I asked one of the guys, "How can I be like you all?" One of them answered, "Just ask Jesus into your heart."

Immediately I prayed, "Jesus, if You are real, come into my heart and forgive me for all that I have ever done wrong." When I went to bed that night everything seemed normal, but when I woke up the next morning, there was a marked difference. I knew it right away. I felt as though things had become lighter. I felt light headed, peaceful, and joyful. All day the peace of God was upon me. It was a peace I'd never experienced before in my life. Can you imagine what it was like for a hardened criminal like me to experience peace for the first time in my life? It was incredible. I knew Jesus Christ was real and that He is alive and was just waiting to help me.

THANK GOD, I AM SAVED!

That night as had become our custom, these Christian inmates and I all knelt to pray. As we knelt, I thought, "Now that I know Jesus Christ is real, what would happen if I really prayed this prayer with my whole heart and asked Jesus to come into my heart?" I said that prayer again, this time omitting "If You are real," and just sincerely asked Jesus Christ to come into my heart and be my Savior. When I did, it seemed as though all of Heaven came down. I broke and began to weep and cry. When I got up off my knees, I knew that Jesus was alive and that He had saved me. For the first time in my life, I felt clean on the inside.

I couldn't believe the change that had taken place in my heart. When I woke up the next morning, I had brand new thoughts. I didn't want my old way of life; all I wanted was to know more about Jesus Christ, this wonderful Savior who had saved me. I was so thankful to God to be saved! A personal relationship with Jesus Christ was what I had been looking for all of my life, and just hadn't known it. You see, salvation is a supernatural act of God. Only God can change your heart and your life. When I got serious with God and prayed and asked Jesus into my heart, my life began to change right then.

This was January 1978. For the first time in my life, I knew that the Bible was the only Word of God. I began to devour the Bible and any Christian literature we could get in the jail. One day we got a book entitled. The New Anointing by Morris Cerillo. In that book, we read about being filled with the Spirit, laying hands on the sick, and casting out devils. When we compared the book with the Scriptures, we found that it was accurate, so we prayed the prayer in the back of the book for the baptism of the Holy Spirit. When you ask Jesus to baptize you in the Holy Spirit, believe that He will and by faith begin to pray in tongues – a heavenly language. The Holy Spirit gives the utterance, but you must step out in faith and began speaking what God gives you supernaturally. (Luke 11:13)

However, in jail at that time, we were not equipped with this understanding. Therefore, after a few weeks of begging God to be baptized in the Holy Spirit with the evidence of speaking in tongues, we received some Voice magazines from The Full Gospel Business Men's Fellowship. God used one of the magazines to stir up my faith. I read the story of a backslider who was filled with the Holy Spirit just by asking God for this Biblical experience. It was at this time that I had my first pity party. I said, "Jesus, I love You just as much as this guy in the magazine. You filled him with the Holy Spirit when he asked You, so why haven't You filled me with the Holy Spirit yet?"

Suddenly the power of God came upon me, and I began to shake uncontrollably, because the power of God was on me so strongly. I went to one of the brother's cell to get some understanding about my shaking. We thought it might be the Holy Spirit, so we went in my cell to pray. As we prayed, the power of God filled my soul and my mouth, and a beautiful heavenly language broke forth. Hallelujah! I was filled with the Holy Spirit!

I felt so different! I received the joy of the Lord, and the love of God filled my heart. I wasn't the same person. Before, my heart had been filled with hate; now it was filled with the love of God, and the power of God filled my life. I'd never experienced anything like that before. When God lives inside of your heart, things are different for you. Your life changes because you've got God on the inside of you! The good things in life that you never had the strength or desire to do, God helps you to do. He gives you supernatural strength and ability to do His will.

The things that you hated to do but didn't have the strength to resist become hateful to you, and God gives you the strength to turn away from them. Drugs were no longer attractive to me. I didn't want to live a life of crime anymore. I realized how much of my life I had wasted doing the devil's plan. Now I wanted to fulfill God's plan for my life. I didn't have the same desires anymore. I didn't want to do things that were wrong and sinful. I wanted to be clean on the inside and live for God.

And with the power of the Holy Spirit in my life – now I had the ability to live right! I learned that the Holy Spirit is the Power Source of God. He gives you the strength and the ability to do what's right.

I stayed in jail from January to May, reading and studying my Bible. In May 1978 I received my first miracle. The prosecutor offered me a plea agreement of four years. This was truly a miracle because I was facing a possible sixty-year term. This was my 23rd arrest, so you can imagine my joy. I knew God was at work in this answering my prayers! I went to the Reception Diagnostic Center of Plainfield, Indiana for two weeks. From there I was sentenced to the Indiana State Prison in Michigan City, Indiana. I arrived in June and immediately joined the prison church. I worked in the kitchen so I had plenty of time for fellowship, prayer, and study.

In June I wrote the judge that sentenced me a letter requesting a shortened sentence or shock probation. I told him I was a different person now, because I had accepted Jesus into my life. Shock probation is when you are released from prison on probation. I knew it was a long shot, but I believed God could do anything. After all, Second Corinthians 5:17 was real to me - I had really changed; I was a new creature in Christ Jesus. I began to take numerous Bible Correspondence Courses. I completed the Salvation Army Advanced Bible Study Course. We began witnessing revival in the prison, with many inmates being born again and set free from the bondages of drug and crime. In July as I meditated on my bunk one morning, Jesus literally appeared to me in my cell and said "William, I want you to build Me a Prison Ministry." After I heard those words, I began to set up a ministry with several other brothers.

We began writing and encouraging other prisoners in the Lord. In August I was called back to court. I was notified that on the strength of my letter to the judge, I was being considered for shock probation.

THE MERCY OF GOD

I was learning the ways of the Holy Spirit and how to follow Him in faith, trusting Him for everything. The judge told me I would stay in the county jail until the court received my prison records. While in the county jail, there were many miracles of salvation among the inmates there. I went to court five times from August to October. At my last court appearance, there was much testimony on my behalf about how I'd changed, but the prosecutor also had a lot to say against me.

Finally the judge said, "Mr. Prosecutor, I'm going to grant Mr. Bumphus shock probation on the grounds that I believe he is a born-again Christian." On that October evening, I left the Marion County Jail to go begin building Jesus a Prison Ministry. I didn't know the first thing about building a Prison Ministry. In fact, I didn't know anything about anything. Everything was new to me. I was living a brand-new life for the first time with the love of God in my heart and the power of the Holy Spirit in my life. Everything was so clean and pure.

I went to my mother's house, knowing I could stay there for a week. I had not been baptized in water yet, so Sunday we all went to a church. At the close of service, I mentioned my desire to be baptized. After much debate concerning tradition, I was told I could be baptized the following week. I had a rough week with no fellowship and nothing to do, so I began to go on the streets passing out tracts. The Holy Spirit led me to a Christian brother who had been in jail with me. It was Friday, and I found out this brother was going to his uncle's church. I went with him on Saturday to a Pentecostal, devil-casting-out, tongue-talking, Spirit-filled church. What a glorious time we had in the Lord! I was baptized in water and joined the church.

In the meantime, the woman I'd married while I was on the run from the law had been running around with other men while I was in prison. When I was released from prison, she said she was going to get a divorce. The marriage had only lasted a little over a year.

GOD'S REWARD
FOR FAITHFULNESS

I began faithfully attending a Spirit-filled church. I'd been going to the church for about six months, when I met the woman who would be my future wife. She attended that same church. This woman was always sitting up in the front during church, always deeply involved in the service. We began to go witnessing together. I noticed that she was a strong, bold Christian.

When I was in jail, I had prayed for God to bless me with a wife who was a strong, bold Christian. It was a joy to see God answering my prayers. We were engaged and began making wedding plans. We went out sharing Jesus whenever we got a chance. One day prior to our wedding after we returned from witnessing, we noticed a group of children on the street corner. On closer observation, we noticed that the children were hovering over a child who was lying in the street. The children standing there were my fiance's children. The child lying in the street was her five-year-old, who had been hit by a car. It was a hit-and-run; the car just kept on going.

As the ambulance turned the corner to get the child, the little girl, LaVeda, died. We buried her, and things were really rough, as you can imagine. I didn't have a job. Juanita, my fiance', was on welfare. Death had struck, and the church condemned us, because I had been married before. My fiance' Juanita, already had children. She had never been married. The church said God killed the baby to judge us because I'd been married before. But the Bible says that when Jesus comes into your heart old things are passed away and all things become new.

I knew Jesus wasn't holding against us what had happened in our old lives before we'd met Jesus. Therefore, Juanita and I got married anyway. I began visiting and corresponding with people in the jails, including prisoners in the Indiana Women's Prison. I was working part time trying to make ends meet, and Juanita had already given birth to our first son and was now pregnant with twins.

THE BEGINNING
OF OUR MINISTRY

On the advice of a Baptist minister we'd helped in the ministry, Jesus Inside Prison Ministry was incorporated and officially became a non-profit organization in October 1981. In 1981 the twins were born two months premature and died. One lived for a little over a week before dying. Perplexed, we still could not blame God, even though this is what we had been taught. A local pastor was one of the first people used by God to assure Juanita and me of God's call on our lives. This pastor had once been a disk jockey at a popular radio station. He became a strong supporter of our ministry and still is to this day. He referred us to a Christian Television Station were I might be able to share my testimony. It was at this television station (WHMB channel 40) that a guest minister had a word of prophecy about the recent deaths of our children.

In this prophecy, we learned that God is not a killer, but that Satan comes to steal, kill, and destroy (John 10:10). I can't tell you the joy in knowing who your enemy is and how to stand against him! Finally after writing proposals, which amounted to wasting time and paper, Jesus spoke to me again saying, "I will raise up businessmen to support this ministry."

In 1982 we opened up a storefront to give clothing and food to inner-city residents. Shortly afterward we also began to hold church services, and Faith Center Church International was born. God was faithful to His Word and began to raise up Christian businessmen to support this ministry. The ministry continued to grow and more prison doors began to open, a little here – a little there.

Things didn't happen just because we were saved and had the call of God on our lives. (Juanita had been saved and called to preach five years before I met her). We had to seek God and obey His Word. But God was true to His Word, and He helped us, just as He'd promised. I strongly share with prisoners the need to take advantage of their situation, and use the time to get the Word deep down on the inside of them. They will need the strength of that Word built into their spirit when they get out of prison.

They will need a solid relationship with Jesus, so they can know how to escape all the snares Satan will try to set for them when they are released. But with God on their side, they do not need to fall prey to Satan and his wiles of drugs, deception, sin, and crime

JESUS IS YOUR ANSWER

I've shared with you some of the more hurtful moments of my past to get your attention so you can see that Jesus Christ is real. If you're not saved – if you've never been born again – Jesus will be your Savior today and save you from a life of sin and crime, just as He saved me. When I say that you need the Word of God more than anything, I mean it. It doesn't matter if you are in prison now or have never been locked up – no one can help you, like Jesus.

The grace of God and the Word of God have kept me from going back into my old lifestyle. As I write this presently I'm traveling to prisons all over the country and has traveled to Lagos, Nigeria 5 times and has begun a prison ministry there.. God has been faithful!

We also have a growing fellowship where believers are actively involved in prison ministries and other outreaches. We send hundreds of pounds of free literature to prison chaplains and prisoners every year.

We also have a Aftercare/Reentry Facility called Jesus House. It was a nursing home but now we use it to help men coming out of prison to get reestablished in the free world. WE can house 50 men.

There is genuine revival going on in prisons! The prison population is growing in relation to crime. We have the answer – His Name is Jesus!

One hears countless stories of men getting out of prison only to commit more crimes. But there is another side of the coin, which I represent. When Jesus changes your heart, you no longer want a life of crime, sin, and drugs because you're recreated in His image.

Testimonies similar to mine are typical for hundreds of men like myself – men who met Jesus in prison and are now free, and busy serving Jesus. I have written this testimony so that Jesus may be glorified. The Bible says, "Where sin abounds, grace much more abounds." This grace is abounding in the prisons of this country. I have been out of prison now more than thirteen years.

Since my release I have not shot dope, smoked dope, stolen anything, or had a drink. The reason I haven't is that Jesus Christ is real; He lives inside my heart, and His Word works. Juanita and I have five grown children and ten grandchildren, all serving Jesus. Our families have been touched because of Jesus in our lives. On May 30, 1988, my mother went home to be with Jesus. She went to Heaven, because she saw the relationship I had with Jesus and got saved.

GOD IS NO RESPECTER OF PERSONS

Kevyn Cameron is a young man I met about 22 years ago, who also was in prison. He was not in a physical prison, but was imprisoned in homosexuality. All his life to his recollection, he had always been like that. He had never had a normal relationship with a female. He also was involved in a life of crime. He stole on a regular basis and hustled in the street, finally becoming in charge of a house of male prostitution in Chicago, Illinois. He was only twenty years old. While out on a late night date, a potential lover reached into the glove compartment and pulled out a Bible and shared the Gospel with Kevyn, and showed him (through the Scriptures) that homosexuality was a sin, that God loved him, and had a plan for his life. Several months later, alone in the house of male prostitution, Kevyn acted on the Word of God and asked Jesus into his heart.

He moved back to Indianapolis, and began attending a good denominational church. However, the power to set a man free was missing there. A friend invited him to our church and ministry and he began to hear more truths of God's Word. He found out that not only did God want him free from that prison of homosexuality, but God could totally get rid of all the mannerisms as well. Today, Kevyn Cameron is an ordained Minister in our ministry and is also volunteer Chaplain at the Putnamville Correctional Facility in Greencastle, Indiana. He and his wife of the last nineteen years have four lovely children.

Kevyn is also employed by FedEx as an Recruitment Specialist.

38

Truly, He sent His Word and healed them and delivered them from their destructions.

Another person I'd like to share with you is Walter. I met Walter Sealey about fourteen years ago in a prison called Marion Adjustment Center, in St. Mary, Kentucky. Walter was from Louisville, Kentucky. Originally from Georgia, he did well in school and excelled in sports, particularly in football, winning a scholarship. All went well the first year, but due to the death of his mother, Walter turned bitter and dropped out of school. For the next several years, he became heavily involved in the drug trade. He was the head of his own business, and had dope houses in several parts of the country. As a young man, he was also heavily involved in the martial arts, and so he was also an enforcer in his lucrative drug trade. Eventually, as it always does, his time ran out, and he was sentenced to one hundred and twenty years. He was given sixty for the state and sixty for the federal.

Prior to being sentenced, he had given his life to Jesus, and when I met him at the Marion Adjustment Center, he had two years in on the state charge. As the Lord opened the door for me to begin to minister there, we became friends. He had shared that he was a solid Christian and had never really sought God for his freedom, until he began to hear what the Spirit of the Lord was saying through me. He began to search the Scriptures and found out for himself, that Jesus wanted him free to take care of his family and to be a witness for Him.

Four years later, after his sixth year of incarceration, God set him free. Walter has now gone home to be with the Lord and he is greatly missed.

Anthony Gregory's story is the same. Very early in life, he got involved with the gang life, terrifying the neighborhoods in all kinds of gang activities, including doing drive-by shootings. He says his main bondage was not as a gang banger, but as a whoremonger. He just couldn't stop the life of illicit sex. He began to father children at the age of fourteen. At age twenty, he also heard the Gospel and was delivered. He's been married to the same woman now for over fourteen years and has taken care of all of his children. He travels to the prisons with me regularly, as does Kevyn. Anthony Gregory is now pastoring a church in Indianapolis. God can set you free from whatever it is – if you'll only trust Him and say what His Word says.

You know, Jesus will change a woman's life, too, if she will trust Him. Listen to what Jesus has done for my wife, Juanita.

SISTER JUANITA'S PERSONAL TESTIMONY

Before I got saved, my mind from a very early age was fixed on men. I was always fantasizing about how I wanted my life to be with a man. My fantasy was like my life, every time you look around I had someone new. My fantasy was with someone new. I didn't like school whatsoever. So really my mind was not on schoolwork or getting an education. From an early age I wanted to have a house full of children. I had an aunt that did, and my grandmother did. I didn't have my first child until I was seventeen, and when I did get started having children I couldn't stop. I have had eight, and three of them are in heaven. Now I have five, "Glory to God" still on this earth.

When I first started wanting to have children, I'm glad I didn't, because I was in a foster home where I stayed for eight years. So they would have taken my children away from me and put them in a foster home, or up for adoption. I "was fast as lightning," as people use to say. I started smoking at nine; drinking, popping pills, smoking reefers at, I guess, twelve!!

At eleven, I had moved back with my mother. I was about four when I was taken away. There were seven of us, and six of us were placed in foster homes when we were taken away. I think my older brother stayed with my aunt. About time I moved with my mother, I was smoking, wrapped up in men (or boys). That was my life for years, and booze. I wasn't on hard drugs. If someone would tell me different pills made me high, I'd take them. I smoked reefers, and was addicted to them. Cussing, nightclubing, partying, stealing, selling my body or giving it away, fighting – everything you can name, I was doing from an early age.

Then I began to have flashbacks at eighteen. Tripping off acid, I guess that was put in marijuana. I felt like I was going to jump out windows. And I began to start having hallucinations and was paranoid, thinking that people were after me. I was in a tremendous amount of fear of everything. I couldn't love, and take care of my children right, and the doctor couldn't help me. The pastor didn't understand what was going on. My life was weird and wild. Asking for the Bible, I called out to God. I needed to know how to be saved.

Before I got saved, all I liked to read was "True Confessions" or "Archie" comics. Other books were no interest to me. I did read my horoscope from the newspaper every day. Then I got saved through my half brother, who witnessed to me. He had witnessed to me before, but I didn't wish to listen, so I rejected him and the good news of the Gospel of Jesus, he was giving me. But during the changes I was going through, I had tried everything else; Mama, doctor, preacher (who told me to get a job). Finally, I listened to my brother and the gospel, he once again presented to me. This time I accepted Jesus as my Lord and my Savior. I was immediately filled with the Holy Ghost. I now speak with other tongues as the Spirit of God gives me utterance. I was called to preach six months later. Glory to God, what can I say?

The devil was still trying to take my mind, but Jesus said "No you don't. I have work for her to do." The devil wanted to put me in a mental hospital. But, God is my witness, I was having a nervous breakdown and Jesus rescued me, before Satan took over my mind completely. Noises frightened me, scary movies made me scared. I couldn't sleep. When I got saved, my mind still needed some working on. You've heard the saying "the mind is a terrible thing to waste." Well, Jesus came, or let's say I received Him, in my life, just in time. I didn't know how to renew my mind.

Renew means : 1. to make new, fresh or strong, again; to restore as to renew the furnishings of something. 2. To begin again, to resume, as they renewed their effort to put in a fresh supply, to replace. 3. to continue in force for a fresh period, to extend, as to renew a lease. I'm glad that our life, our spirits, our minds are repairable, only through the washing and regeneration of the Word of God. Well when I got saved, yes, I stopped cussing, fighting, drinking, different drugs, and even sex. I was truly born again.

The Bible says, "Be ye transformed by the renewing of your mind, that ye may prove what is that good, and acceptable, and perfect, will of God." So, that means getting in the Word of God, and getting the Word of God in you. That was hard for me because I never liked to read much. As I said, I only read comics and true stories. I could read the Bible, but not that well when I got saved. I'd stumble over words and be so embarrassed, not realizing that many were in that same situation with reading. They just tried to hide it.

But I was a preacher and the preacher would read Scriptures often. Well, it was other preachers that couldn't read as well as me. I didn't know then. We were only taught to read the Holy Bible, no other book. Well, that was fine with me; I didn't like reading anyhow and I could barely read the Holy Bible. Who likes to do something they can't do or understand? You know my father couldn't read. I don't know if he ever went to school at all, but he was blessed with excellent jobs at LinkBelt, and worked for the city. Jesus blessed him. We used to say he had nine lives, because we thought he was wicked and never could die. But he's dead now. My brother that led me to Jesus and I ministered to him before he died. He never did a thing for us. My mother had seven children by him, that we know of. Well, anyway, Jesus spared his life.

Because I still had some problems with reading, I wasn't getting enough word and wasn't reading enough. When I got saved I had only been to a Catholic, a Spiritualist and mostly Baptist churches, so I didn't know about the different voices in the world, or that the devil speaks to you. Yes, I had heard people say, "The devil made me do it." I didn't know that we could be influenced by Satan to do wrong, or even influenced by God to do good. I don't know what was really running through my mind. I know that when I wanted to stop cussing and fighting my mother I couldn't. I knew I was hurting her and I would be sorry for it and sometimes apologize to her. But, I couldn't stop. It seemed like a greater force was driving me to do it.

When I begin to have flashbacks from tripping off acid, I wanted to stop smoking reefers and popping pills. Yet, I'd find myself drawn to reefers and it would start the reaction of paranoid all over. I would see, and would get a feeling that the person I was with was trying to kill me, and I'd be running from them, jumping out of cars and such. At first while smoking it, I'm feeling good, but then all of a sudden, boom!! I needed to be free, but how? I called on God. I kept calling. Thank Jesus, He answered! Yes I still wanted to have fun, be with my friends, hang out with my cousins and have a good time, but destiny was calling, "Come, before it is too late." I had promised my cousin's wife I'd start going to church, but I kept putting it off, still wanting to play. I didn't want to jump out of anyone's window, but that's how I would feel.

Something deep, a strong driving force was pulling me to

43

do something weird like that, but I'd stop to pray to God because I had heard about Jesus from a little child. I remember as a little child, I saw a little child I guess, (I thought at first it was a little angel) but they say there are no little angels. When I was about two or three years old, before I was taken away from my mother, I saw it flying over above me as I was crawling up the steps. I remember hearing other children upstairs playing.

No, I don't know how true it is, but I read in a book where someone said that some child-like angels do make a visit to this earth. We can't see them really. I believe it was not in Rebecca Springer's book, but Gordon Lindsay mentions it in his book, a lady named Marietta A. Davis who had a visited heaven.

Maybe it was a bigger angel, but I was a baby myself, and then that is how I saw it. That's how it was shown to me. Maybe it was a baby being taken out of the world on it's way to heaven. I can't explain it, it could have been just a figment of my imagination. I know that the angels guarding over me and my family are huge full grown ones.

I remember when I lost my five year old daughter, who got struck and killed by a car in 1979, I was by my fireplace crying and feeling sad and I remember hearing her voice saying "Don't cry, Mommy, I love you." I felt much better. I remember when I had gotten saved, I came into the church in time to meet a lady, before she died. When we went to her funeral, I heard her voice say, "Sister Nita" (that's what most people call me) "I see your name written around up here in heaven." I rebuked it, when we got home and I told the pastor's wife, she told me that she thought what was said to me was beautiful. I'll always remember that.

Anyway, I didn't know how to hear God, or resist the devil's voices. So when I got saved it was these two forces trying to motivate my mind, my heart (which is my spirit) and body. Once after I got saved, I heard a voice say Satan is going to mess with me seven times as much. I rebuked that and found out it was Jesus. **"THANKS BE UNTO GOD THAT ALWAYS CAUSES US TO TRIUMPH IN CHRIST AND MAKETH MANIFEST THE SAVIOR OF HIS KNOWLEDGE BY US IN EVERY PLACE."** When I first got saved I wanted to serve Jesus so badly, I wanted to please Him. So I was willing to do whatever it took to please Him. I didn't know about salvation. I wanted to be perfect, because I was scared to die and go to hell. I didn't want to go back to having those flashbacks and at the same time Satan was trying to kill me or take my mind. He was trying to stop me from serving God. So one day he told me to stand in the middle of the street and holler out loud, "Jesus." Well I was not a little hesitant, but a lot hesitant. The devil was working on me overtime, but I was determined to be like Jesus. My mother had her beauty shop at 34th street off Illinois here in Indianapolis.

He wanted me to holler it out there. I didn't, so he said well go in the bathroom in the back of the shop. I'm sitting in there and he said to holler out "Jesus" in here as loud as you can. I'm thinking it's Jesus. I messed up outside but he's giving me another chance. I'm hesitant, but I finally get up enough nerve to do it. I did it. He said, now when you go out there and they ask you what was that all about tell them Jesus told me to do it. I know my mother was embarrassed. I went out (I was embarrassed, too, but I felt I had to obey Jesus). I sat down, everybody kept working, didn't look at me. I sat a few minutes. No one asked me about the ordeal in the back. So it came to me to ask them if they heard me. My mother said "Yeah." I said Jesus told me to do that. She said, "Yeah, some woman said Jesus told her to kill her son, too." Well to me, they just didn't understand.

Remember, I'm just getting saved, I'm nineteen if that will help any. Well then in the same day I was told to holler in the street, the bathroom, after that my next test was to go across the street to the beauty supply place. Now on my way I was told by this same spirit to throw a handful of change in the middle of the street, 34th and Illinois, and then go pick it up. If you knew Illinois street, it was extremely busy then. I didn't want to, but I managed to throw it at the curb. Thank Jesus. I then picked it up. I know my mother and all were watching, wondering what I was going to do next. I thank Jesus I lived to get to church that night and explained to the pastor what had happened. I heard later some children said that woman has escaped from a mental hospital.

The pastor said to me, "No, you are not crazy." Then he explained to me about the devil telling me to do that trying to kill me, confuse me, something on that order. That's when I begin to learn about the voices in this world – the battles in the mind. Even though I like to hear the preacher preach, I hated teaching as I did in school. Just give me about fifteen minutes of preaching and whooping and I felt good. That's all my attention could stand. But if you went over the fifteen minutes, I was ready to go.

I use to hate teaching because it took so long. I wasn't the only one like that. I was used to being in a Baptist church, the choir singing, preaching 15 minutes, and announcements which was fine then off to my same daily life.

To me those three temptations remind me of when Jesus was tempted after he was baptized and out in the wilderness fasting and praying. The hollering in the street, hollering in the back room of my mother's shop, throwing the money in the street and picking it up (Satan saying throw it in the middle of the busy street and then pick it up).

As far as education is concerned, Smith Wigglesworth didn't read, until after he got saved, and then just read the Bible. I think William Branham didn't read at all. But God used them very greatly in their walk with Him. I could read, but not like I wanted to. I didn't want to miss a word, if you miss a word, it would throw me back, because I felt as if I had failed.

Thank Jesus, I've come a long way. I remember one day on a radio broadcast we were doing, when a group of ladies were on with me and I was reading and missed a word (live on the radio). Well, that was a few years ago, and I was so embarrassed. I said I had word-fright, and I did, because I read the Scripture before them. An older lady friend of mine, Sister Gaynell Hudson, taught me to say you don't have to prove anything. Now, if I miss it, I miss it. I have learned to go on. I am thankful for what I do know. Now I love to read, read fast, read to people, and study the Word, because I met my husband, who read all the time and he'd tell me about great people that were used by Jesus. Kathryn Kuhlman, Aimee McPherson, Smith Wiggleworth and others. He told me all about the different books he had read about them. So that got me reading more. When you read your Bible more, you enjoy it more. My husband, Pastor William Bumphus, has always loved to listen to Christian tapes. Finally, after years, I enjoy them. I'm believing Jesus for a teaching ministry on television eventually. I believe He puts desires in our hearts, so that we can do more studying and reading. I didn't know I always had the ability to do something for Jesus. I had to get my mind clear from all the past junk that was in there. I had to be trained, but I had no one to help train me. No one had any patience to understand what was going on, so they couldn't help. Their answer was, "Just pray," or their first thought is, "She has a serious mental problem." Well I tell you, if I did, Glory to God, I'm healed by the stripes of Jesus! He's a mind regulator, and a heart-fixer.

He sent Pastor Bumphus and that really helped me. He was speaking in tongues all the time and tried to get me to. I fought it for a while, but I began to speak out. I told him he wasn't to read any other books, but the Bible. He kept reading them and now I'm reading other books, too. He was passing out tracts, I told him that wasn't what I was taught. Now I write tracts. He's always been a teacher and it took me years to get used to it. But glory to God, I love teaching. I'm a teacher now myself and love to teach.

I look at anointed, called people teaching on television now, and I'm amazed at how far I have come. I say, Thank Jesus. The Bible says in I Corinthians 1:25- 29: **"BECAUSE THE FOOLISHNESS OF GOD IS WISER THAN MEN AND THE WEAKNESS OF GOD IS STRONGER THAN MEN. FOR YE SEE YOUR CALLING BRETHREN, HOW THAT NOT MANY WISE MEN AFTER THE FLESH, NOT MANY MIGHTY, NOT MANY NOBLE ARE CALLED! BUT, GOD HATH CHOSEN THE FOOLISH THINGS OF THE WORLD TO CONFOUND THE WISE. AND GOD HATH CHOSEN THE WEAK THINGS OF THE WORLD TO CONFOUND THE THINGS WHICH ARE MIGHTY. AND BASE THINGS OF THE WORLD, AND THINGS WHICH ARE DESPISED, HATH GOD CHOSEN, YEA, AND THINGS WHICH ARE NOT TO BRING TO NOUGHT THINGS THAT ARE THAT NO FLESH SHOULD GLORY IN HIS PRESENCE."**

I am so glad no one could help me; Mama, teachers even the church people that wanted me to be like what they wanted me to be. I can say, I'm God's woman. He saved me. He called me to preach after I was saved. He didn't care what anyone thought, or what it looked like, or how unlearned and ignorant I might have seemed. He saw what He could do with a young girl of nineteen, who was an outcast, "hopeless" to all kinds of people, including friends. He saw in me potential that no one else tried to see. Acts 4:13 says, **"NOW WHEN THEY SAW THE BOLDNESS OF PETER AND JOHN, AND PERCEIVED THAT THEY WERE UNLEARNED AND IGNORANT MEN, THEY MARVELLED AND THEY TOOK KNOWLEDGE OF THEM, THAT THEY HAD BEEN WITH JESUS."**

You know, I'm not perfect and I haven't arrived. But I thank Jesus, I have come so far in my life. From near having a nervous breakdown, to seeing Jesus' plan for me, being a preacher and teacher of the gospel of Jesus. May Jesus bless you. If you have never received Jesus into your life, as your personal Lord and Savior, I would love to lead you to Him. Confess with your mouth the Lord Jesus, and believe in your heart that God hath raised Him from the dead and thou shalt be saved. **"FOR BY GRACE ARE YE SAVED THROUGH FAITH AND THAT NOT OF YOURSELVES IT IS THE GIFT OF GOD LEST ANY MAN SHOULD BOAST "(NOT OF WORKS)** Eph. 2:8.

Come unto Jesus, just as you are, nasty, stinky and all filthy, messed up, abused, sad, tormented, hurting, disappointed, troubled, drunk, high, naked, destitute, criminally insane, a liar, broken-hearted, lover of yourself. Everybody that will; Come to Jesus, before it is everlasting too late. Time is getting very short, and running out quick.

Today is the day of salvation. Tomorrow might not come to you on this earth. Make your decision now. Heaven or hell, choose life, not death, blessings not cursing, Jesus not the devil. Jesus has a future for you – to do good to you, not evil. To give you the best. Our Heavenly Father knows what you have need of, before you ask. Call out to him. He'll hear and answer. He's not willing that any should perish, but wants all to come to repentance. It's the goodness of the Lord that leadeth thee to repentance. Accept His salvation in your life today.

THREE MURDERERS
LOVED BY GOD

When we are born again, we stop being sinners, but are called "Saints." Does that mean that we will never sin? No, it means that we are not sinners, but saints. The difference is that before you and I were born again, we lived to sin. Now that we are born again, we literally become a new person. As we get into the Word, we will begin to think and act like it. However, the Word is true, whether we act like it, or not.

That is where our faith must stand. Not in our experiences, not in our understandings, but in the fact that God cannot lie. If He said it in the Word, then it's true.

Again, when you came to prison, you were not saved. You were a sinner and dangerous as a sinner. Now that you are born again, according to II Corinthians 5:17, you are a new person. You are not a sinner any longer, but you are a saint. Therefore, God does not deal with you as a sinner, but as a saint and a person that has changed. The Bible clearly shows us this in the lives of many men, but for the sake of time and space, we will only look at three prominent men in the Bible and notice their transformation, and God's attitude towards them.

Our first study is of Moses. Almost everyone is familiar with his story. I want to comment on a verse of Scripture about Moses that is just right for the concept you must understand to get your miracle. God changes people and does not hold their past against them.

In Exodus 2:12 we read about Moses. "And he looked this way and that way, and when he saw that there was no man, he slew the Egyptian, and hid him in the sand." Moses clearly killed this man and then hid his body. He also went back to Pharaoh's house as though he had not done a thing. It was only when he went out the next day that he found out that someone had observed his crime of murder. (verse 13) What did Moses do?

He fled for his life into the desert. After forty years in the desert, we see God calling Moses to go back to Egypt to set His people free. As you read through the whole account of Moses' life, you will not find one time where God brings up his past, or tells Moses that he can't use him, because of his past. No, on the contrary, we see God not accepting Moses' excuses, and God uses this "murderer" to give us the first five books of the Bible. What happened? I believe that Moses had plenty of time to reflect upon the crime that he had committed during his time in the desert. I believe that

50

he had Godly sorry for his crime, and I believe that when he acted upon the Word that God gave him at that burning bush, the old Moses died. God then used him mightily.

Let's look at another murderer. His name is David. (I Samuel -1 Kings 2:46)

You know the story of how David should have been at war, but was at the palace instead, and saw Bathsheba washing and desired her. You know how he plotted to have her husband Uriah killed, and how the Prophet Nathan confronted him. Here again is a classic example of the Grace of God. David had committed a sexual sin, and had Uriah killed. But yet, I see the Word of God saying in Acts 13:22, that David was a man after God's own heart. What? Yea. All have sinned, but when we are truly repentant. God forgives and does not hold our sins against us. (Hebrews 10:17) Psalms 51 is the prayer of David's heart. He was truly repentant, and God forgave his sins, and used him and worked miracles on his behalf.

Lastly, how can we ever forget Paul? In Acts 9:1, it talks about his threatenings and slaughters. In Acts 9, he does not have Jesus on his mind. He's on his way to carry out some more crimes against God's people, but the Church was praying. They were praying according to Matthew 5. They were blessing their enemy and God arrested Paul on the Damascus road. Notice, as you read the 9th chapter of Acts, that three days after Paul's conversion, he is being used of God and was continually used throughout the New Testament. In fact. if God used Paul, a slaughterer, to write three fourths of the New Testament, He can use you.

Notice that it didn't take God long to forgive Paul and to use him. It will not take Him long to forgive you and use you as well, when you totally turn your life over to Him.

But, there is one thing that can be a big block to God's changing you and that is – holding on to your past.

FORGET THE PAST

Philippians 3:12-14 states, "NOT THAT I HAVE ALREADY ATTAINED, OR AM ALREADY PERFECTED; BUT I PRESS ON, THAT I MAY LAY HOLD OF THAT FOR WHICH CHRIST JESUS HAS ALSO LAID HOLD OF ME. BRETHREN, I DO NO COUNT MYSELF TO HAVE APPREHENDED; BUT ONE THING I DO, <u>FORGETTING THOSE THINGS WHICH ARE BEHIND</u> AND REACHING FORWARD TO THOSE THINGS WHICH ARE AHEAD. I PRESS TOWARD THE GOAL FOR THE PRIZE OF THE UPWARD CALL OF GOD IN CHRIST JESUS."

So, I'm not saying this, because I've got everything together. I'm saying this, because it's the truth of God's Word! I have to abide by it, also. And there are marriages and ministries and all kinds of things that people cannot get into, because they cannot forget their past. They can't have a successful marriage, because every man or every woman in their lives dogged them out. So they're in marriage and they can't trust a man, or can't trust a wife, but it's not based on the future; it's not based on God's Word because God told you to trust them in spite of the past.

Look at Philippians 4:8, "FINALLY BRETHREN [saints], WHATSOEVER THINGS ARE TRUE [not what you think is the truth], WHATSOEVER THINGS ARE HONEST, WHATSOEVER THINGS ARE JUST, WHATSOEVER THINGS ARE PURE, WHATSOEVER THINGS ARE LOVELY, WHATSOEVER THINGS ARE OF A GOOD REPORT, IF THERE BE ANY VIRTUE AND IF THERE BE ANY PRAISE, THINK ON THESE THINGS."

Satan uses our past to destroy our future. Why? He does that because he doesn't know our future. The Bible says, "EYE HAS NOT SEEN, NOR EAR HEARD, NOR HAVE ENTERED INTO THE HEART OF MAN THE THINGS WHICH GOD HAS PREPARED FOR THOSE WHO LOVE HIM." (I Cor. 2:9). But it goes on to say that the Holy Spirit knows these things (v.10), Satan doesn't know them.

God knows your future. And the Bible says He has purposed for you to have a blessed future. But the only way Satan can keep you from having this blessed future is to keep your mind of your past. If you constantly think about the past, the past will cause you to have no future. After I got this message, I was reading in Mac Hammond Ministries Magazine and he says that out of the poor people, that is, people who are in poverty, 99% of them will never get out of poverty. Ninety-nine percent of people in poverty will never get out! Why? Because they remember, they cannot forget what it felt like to have nothing.

And so instead of them living in their future, they are living their lives based on their past. So instead of them tithing a dime of every dollar, the poverty mentality is, "Now, that's stupid; I need twenty dollars, and he's talking about tithing the twenty. Give up the twenty? No way! Now how in the world are you going to give something, when you don't have anything!" This is a poverty mentality and these people don't tithe, and don't give an offering on a regular basis. And then they don't expect for prosperity to really come to pass. Why? It's because they can't forget their past. They can't forget they never did have enough money. They can't forget what that felt like. Sure, in their minds they think they're going to do better. Well, how are they going to do better? They think, "I'll save my money and not give tithes and not give offerings and not give any special offerings." But all they're doing is living in the same area of defeat.

In the area of husband and wife relationships, she remembers when he did this, or he remembers when she did that; so, they don't have a future and their marriage is not blessed. But, in spite of acting this way, we call ourselves Christians. We call ourselves "faith people." We "believe the Word!" Well, we really don't believe it because our actions say we don't, and by our thought life we don't either. Because if we believe the Word, we know the Word says that everyone can change! We say we are faith people, and yet we say, "I'll believe it when I see it!" But no, we are faith people, "we believe that we receive; I call things that be not as though they were!"

But when it comes to the real deal, we really believe, "I'll believe it when I see it. When he acts right, then I'll believe that God has changed him. When she acts right, then I'll believe that God has changed her." Well, that thinking just nullified your faith. You're not living by faith; you're walking by sight. You are basing what you see on how it used to be. So you have not forgotten the past. And because you have not forgotten the past, you don't have any future.

I might as well help you, you know. Some of you have been in prison fifteen, twenty years and you still haven't forgotten the past. Forgetting the past is no easy thing to do, you just can't turn it off. There's only one way you can forget the past. First of all, you've got to make up your mind, "I'm through thinking like that." You've got to make up your mind, and then you've got to fight those thoughts off. And it's hard! It's hard because thoughts are the only entrance that Satan has into your life. That's the only way Satan can stop you from becoming successful. The only way Satan can stop you from becoming successful is through your thought life.

If Satan can keep you down on his level, you'll never have anything, because forgetting the past is God's system. You have to play it the way God says it. And so it you are constantly thinking, "I remember when," you are harboring hurt! You think, "I don't want anybody to talk to me and hurt me like that again! I don't want to feel like that again!" So, you guard yourself to stay safe. You show People only what you want them to see! You think, "they'll never see the real me." What are you doing? You are living a lie. So nobody knows you, and you don't even know you. Why? It is because you are harboring past failures.

We want revival and it begins with us in our hearts. But

54

we have to get our hearts right. Proverbs 13 :12 says, **"HOPE DEFERRED MAKETH THE HEART SICK. BUT WHEN THE DESIRE COMETH, IT IS A TREE OF LIFE."**

A more modern translation of that says, **"HOPE DEFERRED [or disappointed], CAN BREAK YOUR HEART."**

What that means is that disappointments in your past broke your heart. You know, all of those boyfriends you had before you got saved, or all of those girlfriends you had before you got saved. You remember the many times that you thought they cared for you and they didn't. They used you and played on you. They disappointed you and that hurt in your heart. It broke your heart. When we look back on it we think it was love, but it was really disappointment. Like when you are going with that person when you think everything is okay, and then you turn around and find out that they are having sex on you!

Let's be honest. What did it do to you? It broke your heart, and you wanted to kill them, or somebody. Then you think, "I'll get even with them, let me find me somebody! I'll get even with them. I'll go with their best friend! Do me like that, huh? I'll show them how it feels!" What are you doing? You were disappointed in them. You didn't think they'd do you like that. Now, after a while, you just expect that they all are going to do you like that anyway. Hope is deferred. Then you form these mind thoughts, "there's no good guys; there's no good women. Man, I wouldn't trust her around that corner!" Hope was deferred. Then, after you are born again, you get into a relationship with another born again person, but you haven't forgotten the past. You know what I'm talking about, you're living there now.

So, the man says, "I love you."

You think, "Hmm, I've heard that before."

It's the same way with the woman telling the man, "I love you; I'm yours until the end."

"Um-hmm," he thinks, "as long as I'm paying these bills!"

Then some folks are like, "Um-hmm, everything is fine as long as you are paying these bills, but you lose your job, and I'm gone."

Now, that sounds real nice, but it's sin. God didn't say get rid of your husband because he doesn't work. God didn't say get rid of your wife because she won't cook. Yeah, put him out because he isn't working.

What did Paul say in Philippians? He begins to give us some clues to get to the point on how we can forget our pasts. Now once we forget our pasts, God can begin to operate on us and have revival in our hearts. Revival in our hearts means that God is removing all that deadness in your hearts that comes from past hurt. The Bible says "THE WAGES OF SIN IS DEATH."

A lot of Christians are walking around full of sin. We pride ourselves on, "we don't smoke, we don't chew, we don't hang around with folks that do. We don't drink, we don't use drugs. I don't party any more." But we say, "I can't stand her over there. She better not come over here. That church over there isn't right." Yeah, we sit at home and have roast Pastor for dinner today. But we say, "I'm saved." Well, you're saved but you're dead... full of sin. The Bible says to get rid of the sin and the weight that so easily besets you. Beset means to make you miss the mark. God said to get rid of that weight. Look at Galatians 5:1-19, **"THIS I SAY THEN, WALK IN THE SPIRIT AND YOU SHALL NOT FULFILL THE LUST OF YOUR FLESH, FOR THE FLESH LUS-TETH AGAINST THE SPIRIT AND THE SPIRIT AGAINST THE FLESH AND THESE ARE CONTRARY THE ONE TO THE OTHER SO THAT YOU CANNOT DO THE THING THAT YOU WOULD. BUT IF YOU BE LED OF THE SPIRIT YOU ARE NOT UNDER THE LAW. NOW THE WORKS OF THE FLESH ARE MANIFEST WHICH ARE THESE. . .**

Adultery is not a devil. There is no sense in someone lay-ing on hands to cast out a spirit of adultery. There's no truth in the saying, "the devil made me do it." No he didn't. The

Bible says that adultery is a manifestation of you walking in your flesh. So is fornication. Fornication is having sex with anybody that isn't your wife or husband. The devil didn't make you do it. Other works of the flesh are uncleanness, lasciviousness. Lasciviousness is a wretched life that consists of just being off into all kinds of stuff like partying and nightclubing. Saints of God often do these things.

Other works of the flesh are idolatry and witchcraft. Witchcraft is not the work of the devil. All of these are works of your flesh. Satan didn't make you do that. Hatred – "I just hate her, Lord knows I have the right to." Variance, emulations, wrath, strife, seditions, heresies, envyings, murders, drunkenness, revelings and such like of which I tell you before, as I have also told you in time past they which do such things shall not inherit the Kingdom of God!" I didn't write that. Sometimes a person might feel justified. "Well, I remember when that brother did that," or "I remember when that sister did that. So, I'm right to feel like I do." That's justification that comes from the devil. Sure, you're justified and you can feel like that. You can feel hatred and wrath and envy against that individual, but I'm just telling you what the Bible says.

Now, notice there's nothing in that list about smoking. We shout at the adultery – we aren't in adultery. We shout at the fornication – we aren't in fornication. We shout at the drinking – we aren't messing around with any of that stuff. Ok, but what about hatred? What about wrath? What about strife? What about heresies? What about envying? What about them? They're in the same verse. The Bible says that those who do such things will not inherit the Kingdom of God. I'm here to tell you, you aren't going anywhere. Knowing this is what makes you get your house in order. Knowing that you can't walk around with that stuff on the inside is what Paul was saying over here in Philippians, chapter 3.

GOD DIDN'T DO IT

In order to really let go of the past, there's another thing you must know – God didn't do it! Genesis 1:26 says, **"LET US MAKE MAN IN OUR IMAGE, AFTER OUR LIKENESS; AND LET THEM HAVE DOMINION OVER THE FISH OF THE SEA, AND OVER THE FOWL OR THE AIR, AND OVER EVERY CREEPING THING THAT CREEPETH UPON THE EARTH. "** In verse 16 and 17 we read, **"AND THE LORD GOD COMMANDED THE MAN, SAYING, 'OF EVERY TREE OF THE GARDEN THOU MAYEST FREELY EAT. BUT OF THE TREE OF THE KNOWLEDGE OF GOOD AND EVIL, THOU SHALT NOT EAT OF IT. FOR IN THE DAY THAT THOU EAT-EST THEREOF THOU SHALT DIE.'"**

According to these verses God created the earth and He created mankind and He turned the earth over to man. Psalm 115:16 states, **"THE HEAVEN, EVEN THE HEAVENS ARE THE LORD'S: BUT THE EARTH HATH HE GIVEN TO THE CHILDREN OF MEN."**

He told us to go and subdue, control the earth and replenish (fill) the earth. God created earth and gave us dominion, rule, over it, but he also gave us a choice or free will.

Adam and Eve chose willingly to disobey God's voice. They did this by eating the forbidden fruit and when they did, they received the curse of death and destruction upon themselves and the earth. Rom. 8:19-20. God, knowing what their disobedience would bring, could have destroyed Adam and Eve and created another couple who would have obeyed Him; but if He did, He would be guilty of break-ing His own Word. He had given Adam dominion, which included free will. Instead, God had a plan from the foun-dation of the world that in the fullness of time Jesus would redeem, bring man back, to Himself.

God is sovereign, but He has subjected Himself to our will in accordance to His Word. He has to allow us to exercise our free will! I've listened for years and in the past, in the beginning of my salvation, even believed that God was behind the disasters and destructions in the world. I believed that He was using all of these things for His ultimate plans. But as I've studied the word over these 23 years, I've found that these were just religious answers but not the truth of what the New Testament teaches. In Hebrews 8:6 we read, **"BUT NOW HE HAS OBTAINED A MORE EXCELLENT MINISTRY, IN AS MUCH AS HE IS ALSO A MEDIATOR OF A BETTER COVENANT, WHICH WAS ESTABLISHED ON BETTER PROMISES."**

James 1:13 commands, **"LET NO MAN SAY WHEN HE IS TEMPTED (TEMPTED, TESTED, TRIED), I AM TEMPTED OF GOD: FOR GOD CANNOT BE TEMPTED WITH EVIL, NEITHER TEMPTED HE ANY MAN."**

So, disasters, destructions, diseases, do not come from God. The temptations, tests, and trials come from the devil.

Look at Luke 4:2: **"BEING FORTY DAYS, TEMPTED OF THE DEVIL,"** and I Peter 5:8-9 which says, **"BE SOBER, BE VIGILANT; BECAUSE YOUR ADVERSARY THE DEVIL, AS A ROARING LION, WALKETH ABOUT, SEEKING WHOM HE MAY DEVOUR / WHOM RESIST STEADFAST IN THE FAITH . . . "**

Satan is our enemy, not God; if we are not convinced of this, then we cannot resist him steadfast in the faith! Our adversary is the devil, the flesh and the world – not God. Many will say that God is still in control and Satan couldn't do anything without God giving him permission. Satan does not need permission to be a devil, he already is! His very nature is death and destruction. God does not give him permission to attack us.

The Bible has been completed and reading through the New Testament, you'll see Jesus constantly warning us that the thief will kill, steal and destroy-John 10:10. He warns us that Satan comes to steal the Word out of our heart, **"SATAN COMETH IMMEDIATELY AND TAKETH AWAY THE WORD**

THAT WAS SOWN IN THEIR HEART" (Mark 4:15).

Jesus warns us that Satan is our enemy. He also has equipped us to triumph over our enemy, always, **"NOW THANKS BE UNTO GOD, WHICH ALWAYS CAUSETH US TO TRIUMPH IN CHRIST"** (2 Corinthians 2:14).

Look at Ephesians 6:10-11, **"FINALLY, MY BRETHREN, BE STRONG IN THE LORD, AND IN THE POWER OF HIS MIGHT / PUT ON THE WHOLE ARMOUR OF GOD, THAT YE MAY BE ABLE TO STAND AGAINST THE WILES OF THE DEVIL."**

No, God is not commissioning, allowing Satan's attack upon mankind. Satan is merely fulfilling Scripture. He's going to wreck havoc, until he's thrown into the lake of fire and brimstone (Rev. 20:1-3, 7-10). As you and I arm ourselves properly with the Word of God, we can be more effective in thwarting and reversing Satan's plans.

WHAT ABOUT JOB?

I hear this question often, when people are trying to blame God for the disasters and diseases of the world. They say things like, God allowed Satan to attack Job and he was a righteous man, so God allows Satan to inflict things upon us. At first reading, this might seem like the case, but further study brings more truth to light.

2 Timothy 2:15 says, **"STUDY TO SHOW YOURSELF APPROVED UNTO GOD . . . RIGHTLY DIVIDING THE WORD OF TRUTH."**

Well, if you can rightly divide the Word of God, then you can wrongly divide it, and in the study of Job, many have wrongly divided it. There were many reasons why things happened to Job that should never happen to New Testament Christians:

#1- Job was not saved!

#2- Job was not filled with the Holy Ghost.

#3- He did not have access to the name of Jesus.

#4- He did not have the Word of God.

#5- Satan had not been judged, neither was he revealed to the Old Testament saints as the destroyer, thief and murderer that He is.

#6- Job walked in fear (Job 3:25).

#7- Finally, Job was under a different covenant.

Under our covenant Satan has been revealed as the person responsible for the evils in this world. He has also been judged and stripped of the power He demonstrated in the Old Testament. I John 3:8 states, **"HE WHO SINS IS OF THE DEVIL, FOR THE DEVIL HAS SINNED FROM THE BEGINNING. FOR THIS PURPOSE THE SON OF GOD WAS MANIFESTED, THAT HE MIGHT DESTROY THE WORKS OF THE DEVIL" (NKJV) and in John 16:11 (NKJV). ". . . THE RULER OF THIS WORLD IS JUDGED"**

God speaks to us through the Apostle Paul in Ephesians 6: 10-18. He lets us know who our enemy is, and how to defeat him in our lives and circumstances. If we know the word and choose to abide by it, we'll experience victory and live the overcoming life. On the other hand, if we choose to live by our own understanding, then we'll walk in defeat. It is imperative that we share the gospel more. People without the knowledge of Christ will always make wrong choices. There is no middle ground. You are either a child of God or a child of the devil. If Jesus is not the Lord of your life, then Satan is in control of your life and circumstances. Without Jesus in one's life, then a person does not have control over the devil.

Whatever you are going through, or this nation is going through, GOD DIDN'T DO IT! Our choices bring disasters or blessings. In Deuteronomy 30:19 states, **"I CALL HEAVEN AND EARTH AS WITNESSES TODAY AGAINST YOU, THAT I HAVE SET BEFORE YOU LIFE AND DEATH, BLESSING AND CURSING: THEREFORE CHOOSE LIFE, THAT BOTH YOU AND YOUR DESCENDANTS MAY LIVE."**

By choosing Jesus and purposing to live according to the Word of God, we strengthen our chances of a long life (Psalm 91) and an abundant life (John 10:10).

I've heard other Christians say that "Word of faith people believe that you will never have tests and trials, if you have enough faith." I know of no teaching which states this. On the contrary, living by faith, by the Word of God, will cause you to be attacked more by the forces of the devil. Mark 4 says that Satan comes to steal the Word, and he does it by the circumstances of life. Regardless of whose camp you're in, we, as Christians cannot escape trials. The victory, however, over your trials and temptations comes only by knowing and walking in the Word of God. I John 5:4-5 says, **"FOR WHATEVER IS BORN OF GOD OVERCOMES THE WORLD. AND THIS IS THE VICTORY THAT HAS OVERCOME THE WORLD OUR FAITH. WHO IS HE WHO OVERCOMES THE WORLD, BUT HE WHO BELIEVES THAT JESUS IS THE SON OF GOD" (NKJV).**

Jesus is our Saviour, our Deliverer. We have nothing to fear. Daily, read your Bible. Daily, spend time with God in prayer and meditation of His Word. Daily, speak His Word into and over your circumstances and you'll always triumph. Jesus loves you, God loves you and you are never alone. If you have not asked Jesus into your heart yet, do it now and allow His peace into your life. In Joshua 1:8 we read, **"THIS BOOK OF THE LAW SHALL NOT DEPART OUT OF THY MOUTH, BUT THOU SHALT MEDITATE THEREIN DAY AND NIGHT, THAT THOUGH MAYEST OBSERVE TO DO ACCORDING TO ALL THAT IS WRITTEN THEREIN. FOR THEN THOU SHALT MAKE THY WAY PROSPEROUS, AND THEN THOU SHALT HAVE GOOD SUCCESS."** Choose Life!

To receive salvation and life, pray the sinner's prayer below out loud:

Dear Heavenly Father,

I come to You in the Name of Jesus. Your Word says, "him that cometh to me I will in no wise cast out." (John 6: 37), so I know that You won't cast me out, but You take me in. I thank You for it.

You said in Your Word "Whosoever shall call upon the Name of the Lord shall be saved" (Rom. 10:13). I am calling on Your Name, so I know that You have saved me now.

You also said, "If thou shalt confess with thy mouth the Lord Jesus, and shalt believe in thine heart that God hath raised him from the dead, thou shalt be saved. For with the heart man believeth unto righteousness; and with the mouth confession is made unto salvation" (Rom. 10:9, 10).

I believe in my heart Jesus Christ is the Son of God. I believe that He was raised from the dead for my justification. And I confess Him now as my Lord, because Your Word says, "with the heart man believeth unto righteousness" and I do believe that in my heart. Therefore, I have now become the righteousness of God in Christ (2 Cor. 5:21).

I am saved! Thank you, Lord!

BAPTISM
by Juanita Bumphus

"What's up with the Baptism in water?" One you're following the footsteps of Jesus. St. Matt. 3:11-17, Mark 1:6-11, Luke3:21-22

How should a Christian be baptized? Buried in water, not sprinkled, not sprayed with water, not even anointed with water in the name of the Father, Son and Holy Ghost. St. John 3:1-8, St. John 1:13, Acts 22:16. Baptism is not the cleansing factor, but proving factor. 1 Peter 3:21, Titus 3:5 Baptism is revelation that you are born again. Acts 8:36-38, Matt. 3:13-17; Matt. 28:18-20, Acts 2:38

Who can be baptized, can backsliders? Ezekiel 3:20; Ezekiel 18:24; Ezekiel 33:13; Rev. 2:4-5

Backsliders are candidates for baptism, wouldn't you think? Babies are not to be baptized, but consecrated. Mark 10:13-16, Luke 2:22.

Why should Christians be baptized? To follow the example of Jesus, to be obedient. Romans 6:3-4

Juanita, my wife, shares with us that baptism is an outward manifestation of salvation. After you are saved, you should receive the water baptism. It's symbolic of the death, burial and resurrection of Jesus. Juanita goes on to say, "I remember when I got saved and got baptized. I had been baptized many times in the past. The first time I was about 5 to 7 years old and then when I got older, only the Lord knows how many other times. But when I repented of my sins and gave Jesus my life, and not just joined a church, there was a difference in my baptism; I stepped in the water and it was cold, it chilled my body, but not my soul. I don't remember feeling any different, but that night when I went to bed, I felt strange and it scared me. I felt something moving up and down on the inside of me. Reminds me now of Star Trek when Captain Kirk gets beamed up. "Beam me up, Scottie, he'd say."

It's that transformation they had from here to there. So that's what it reminds me of now and I'm not afraid but excited about the experience of my new birth. Thank Jesus that now I don't have to get baptized every year to try to find some hope. I've found my hope and new life in Jesus. You should get saved, before you get baptized. I heard someone say, "You can go down a dry devil, and come up a wet devil."

HOLY SPIRIT
by William Bumphus

Luke 11:13, **"IF YE THEN, BEING EVIL, KNOW HOW TO GIVE GOOD GIFTS UNTO YOUR CHILDREN; HOW MUCH MORE SHALL YOUR HEAVENLY FATHER GIVE THE HOLY SPIRIT TO THEM THAT ASK HIM."**

Now that you have asked Jesus into your heart as your personal Savior, you are now a candidate for the gift of the Holy Spirit. You receive the Holy Spirit the same way you received salvation. You simply ask Jesus to fill you with His Spirit and according to Luke11:13, He does.

In Acts 2:4,10:46,19:6; 1 Corinthians 12:10 and 14:5, those that received the Holy Spirit also spoke in tongues. The same will happen to you as you act on the Word of God.

In 1 Corinthians 14, the Bible tells us about tongues and their function in the Church and in our private lives. In Acts 1:8, the Bible lets us know that the Holy Spirit comes to give us power to be a witness for the Lord Jesus. Also in the book of Jude and in Romans 8:26, we see that the Holy Spirit also comes to help us pray. So now that you are born again, ask

God for the Holy Spirit and then believe you receive.

Some say that tongues have passed away, however, the Holy Spirit has not passed away and tongues are a part of His personality. In Acts 2:39, the Bible says concerning the Holy Spirit and tongues, "FOR THE PROMISE IS UNTO YOU, AND TO YOUR CHILDREN, AND TO ALL THAT ARE AFAR OFF, EVEN AS MANY AS THE LORD OUR GOD SHALL CALL."

The Lord is still calling people to be saved and thus the Holy Spirit and tongues are for today.

PRAYER

"AND HE SPAKE A PARABLE UNTO THEM TO THIS END, THAT MEN OUGHT ALWAYS TO PRAY, AND NOT TO FAINT" (Luke 18:1)

Prayer is how we communicate with God and it is also the way He communicates with us. (see John 10) Prayer brings us into the presence of God and allows the Holy Spirit to minister to us and lead and guide us. Matthew 7:7, **"ASK AND IT SHALL BE GIVEN TO YOU, SEEK AND YE SHALL FIND, KNOCK AND THE DOOR SHALL BE OPENED UNTO YOU."**

Jesus also said through the Apostle John in 1 John 5:14-16, **"AND THIS IS THE CONFIDENCE THAT WE HAVE IN HIM, THAT, IF WE ASK ANYTHING ACCORDING TO HIS WILL. HE HEARETH US, AND IF WE KNOW THAT HE HEARETH US, WHATSOEVER WE ASK, WE KNOW THAT WE HAVE THE PETITIONS THAT WE DESIRED OF HIM."**

A crucial part in our receiving from God the answers to our prayers, is praying according to His will. You might ask. How can anyone know the will of God? The answer to that question is very simple. The Word of God is the will of God.

As we learn, read, and study the Bible, we learn more of God's will for our lives. Our prayers then begin to line up with His revealed will for us, and our prayers begin to be answered.

Answering our prayers is one of God's ways of revealing how much he loves us. It also will help to build our confidence in Him and in His Word. Finally, when you pray, pray to God in JESUS name.

"YE HAVE NOT CHOSEN ME, BUT I HAVE CHOSEN YOU, AND ORDAINED YOU, THAT YE SHOULD GO AND BRING FORTH FRUIT, AND THAT YOUR FRUIT SHOULD REMAIN; THAT WHATSOEVER YE SHALL ASK OF THE FATHER IN MY NAME. HE MAY GIVE IT YOU" (John 15:16).

So start everyday with prayer and end everyday with prayer.

READING/STUDY

As stated in the previous chapter, reading and studying your Bible will help you to know the will of God for your life. Knowing God's will and knowing what's in the Bible gives us the power needed to stand against the wiles of the devil. (Ephesians 6:10-18)

Reading the Bible is also the number one way God speaks to us. He speaks to us through His Word. Joshua 1:8 **"THIS BOOK OF THE LAW SHALL NOT DEPART OUT OF THY MOUTH; BUT THOU SHALT MEDITATE THEREIN DAY AND NIGHT, THAT THOU MAYEST OBSERVE TO DO ACCORDING TO ALL THAT IS WRITTEN THEREIN; FOR THEN THOU SHALT MAKE THY WAY PROSPEROUS AND THEN THOU SHALT HAVE GOOD SUCCESS."**

Paul told Timothy in 1 Timothy 4:12-13, **"LET NO MAN DESPISE THY YOUTH; BUT BE THOU AN EXAMPLE OF**

THE BELIEVERS, IN WORD, IN CONVERSATION, IN CHARITY, IN EXHORTATION, TO DOCTRINE." 2 Timothy 2:15, **"STUDY TO SHOW THYSELF APPROVED UNTO GOD, A WORKMAN THAT NEEDETH NOT TO BE ASHAMED, RIGHTLY DIVIDING THE WORD OF TRUTH"**

The above scriptures give us a scriptural foundation for reading and studying the Bible.

There are several different Bible translations available today for those that might have a hard time with the King James Version. I suggest the N.I.V., N.A.S.B., or N.K.J.V.

Begin your Bible reading or study with prayer, asking the Holy Spirit for wisdom and understanding. Begin reading the New Testament, if you are a new Christian. Read the New Testament through several times before you begin to spend a lot of time in the Old Testament.

FELLOWSHIP

"BUT IF WE WALK IN THE LIGHT, AS HE IS IN THE LIGHT, WE HAVE FELLOWSHIP ONE WITH ANOTHER" (I John 1:7).

As believers, we are to have fellowship with other believers. We are not to have constant dealings with those that are not believers. We have to fellowship with each other to strengthen each other. Fellowship with unbelievers will eventually destroy you because they are not traveling on the same road of life as you are.

Romans 10:17, **"SO THEN FAITH COMETH BY HEARING AND HEARING BY THE WORD OF GOD."**

As you fellowship around the Word of God and with God's people, your faith will grow. Find a good church to attend. If you are incarcerated, go to the Christian services. Hang out with those you know to be solid Christians. As you do, you'll notice your own faith growing.

"WHEREFORE, THE RATHER, BRETHREN, GIVE DILI-

GENCE TO MAKE YOUR CALLING AND ELECTION SURE: FOR IF YOU DO THESE THINGS, YE SHALL NEVER FALL" (2 Peter 1:10).

As a prisoner at the Indiana State Prison, I learned these same principles I've just shared with you.

I received the Holy Spirit in the Marion County Jail while awaiting my trial after I had prayed to receive Jesus into my heart as my personal Savior. I began to speak in tongues then and have not ceased since that day. When I was sentenced and arrived at the prison, I read my Bible daily and enrolled in numerous Bible Studies and Correspondence courses (If you need a Bible Correspondence course, please contact the Chaplain's office if you're incarcerated. If the Chaplain cannot help you, please contact my office). The Correspondence courses helped me to study and to learn the Word of God. I prayed everyday. I prayed when I awoke and throughout the day asking Jesus to help me in everything I did.

I began to attend Chapel Services, and Bible Studies and prayer meetings in the church there and met on the yard with other brothers for the sake of fellowship. As we did, we were able to share our faith with others and many more became believers.

Today, as I write this, I've been walking with Jesus now for the last 23 years. I still do the same things as I learned to do there in the prison and I am thoroughly convinced that by doing what the Word says, I have been able to remain free and to be able to be used by the Lord to share the Gospel. I haven't shot dope, drunk any alcohol, stole, or been with any other woman other than my wife for the last 23 years!

2 Peter 1:10 is real! If you do these things, you shall never fall! God wants us to live a life of victory in all areas of our life (John 10:10), however, the devil wants us to live a life of defeat. God has provided a way of escape from the temptations and snares of the devil, but it's only by adhering to His plan.

The Word of God works, but it will only work for us, as

we work it. Just like God doesn't want you to backslide, neither do I. I know this is the reason He has enabled me to write this little book, to help you as you begin your journey with Him.

Many reading this will be leaving prison soon and are wondering about the future. Will I stay out? Will the Word really work for me? To both questions, the answer is YES!

To those incarcerated, stay in the Word. Use this time to grow strong in the Lord. Jesus is on your side.

BELIEVING AND SPEAKING THE WORD

As Prison Evangelists and Prison Ministries, we've done a great job on teaching and preaching the death, burial, and resurrection of Jesus, however, we've fallen short on the rest of the Bible. I believe the same truth that we convey to those who come into our churches should be the same truth that we communicate to prisoners as well. That is, that Jesus came to set the "whole" man free.

In John 8:32, Jesus tells us that the truth will make us free. In verse 31, He lets us know how to obtain that truth. He says, "IF YOU CONTINUE IN MY WORD." I submit to you now, that in order to become free, to get out of what you are in and stay out, you MUST continue in the Word and by doing so, you will come to know the truth as Jesus presents it, and that truth will make you free. Let's examine some truths of God's Word.

Men and women are packed into prisons today and are literally being warehoused. Privatization of prisons is the third fastest growing stock on the stock market. No wonder no one wants to address the cause of this crisis. Everyone knows that the number one cause of the major crime problem is drugs. So why aren't drug treatment centers set up all across the country to deal with this problem? If there were federally and/or state funded treatment centers, we would witness a drastic decline in murders and violent crime. Because there aren't any, substantially, across the country, the only option left is long imprisonment.

I feel very strongly that in this area, we as a church cannot wait on the government. We must open these centers ourselves and give them the real answer to their addictions. In the midst of this apparent billion dollar industry we call "Corrections," there is a mighty move of God prevailing within the prisons, called "Revival!"

Men and women and young people in prisons and youth facilities are turning to Jesus in record numbers. This is wonderful and I stay in an atmosphere of joy because of it. They are doing their time as Christians. However, they are still imprisoned, and for many with too much time.

As I prayed and studied, my question to God was, "How do these men and women become free again to benefit society with the talents and gifts and the new life they now have?" My answer came through the Word and I've been preaching how to get out of prison and stay out ever since.

Since I can only travel so fast and preach just so much, I've decided, with the help of the Lord, to put the meat of that message in printed form because it can travel faster and go into places I might never go.

Our answer to this vital question begins with Psalm 107:20, **"HE SENT HIS WORD, AND HEALED THEM, AND DELIVERED THEM FROM THEIR DESTRUCTION."**

God's method of delivering us and setting us free is through His Word. We must know the Word. I didn't say that we must know what someone says the Word says. We who are seeking for deliverance, must know what the Word says for ourselves.

Many committed, strong, Christian prisoners are still locked up because they do not know the truth. Now I can just hear you saying, "I've been studying my Bible ever since I got locked up, I've got numerous Bible Correspondence Courses, Certificates, and Diplomas, etc." My answer to that is Wonderful! But, sad to say, ninety percent of all you've studied and read is denominational tradition and has taught you that miracles have passed away. Miracles have not passed away, because Jesus is the Miracle worker. If miracles have passed away, then Jesus has.

Most of you whom I'm addressing need a miracle. How can you get a miracle if you don't believe that they are for you? Look at Mark 9:23, **"JESUS SAID UNTO HIM, IF THOU CANST BELIEVE, ALL THINGS ARE POSSIBLE TO HIM THAT BELIEVETH."**

Jesus said in this verse that ALL things are possible to him that can believe. The last time I checked my concordance and my dictionary, ALL still meant ALL. Jesus here was telling this man how he could get a miracle, and He is saying the same thing to you.

Notice what Jesus told Martha, before He raised Lazarus from the dead, **"JESUS SAID UNTO HER, I AM THE RESURRECTION, AND THE LIFE: HE THAT BELIEVETH IN ME, THOUGH HE WERE DEAD, YET SHALL HE LIVE: AND WHOSOEVER LIVETH AND BELIEVETH IN ME SHALL NEVER DIE. BELIEVEST THOU THIS?"** (John 11:25-26)

Notice in verse 27, Martha believed. If you can believe it, you can receive it. Jesus wants to work miracles in your life, but He has to have your help. He can't violate His Word. You have to believe. You might say that God can do what He wants to do, when He wants to do it. So when the Lord gets ready for me to leave, then He'll do it. Now that sounds good, but it is totally incorrect. You will leave that prison when you get ready by activating God's Word in your life and IN YOUR MOUTH. Your miracle comes from acting on the Word.

Let's look at a verse of Scripture that I know some people wish wasn't in the Bible, but it is in the Bible, and in red ink. Mark 11:23, **"FOR VERILY I (Jesus) SAY UNTO YOU,**

THAT WHOSOEVER (you) SHALL SAY UNTO THIS MOUN-
TAIN (that sickness, that sentence or disease, etc.) BE THOU
REMOVED, AND BE THOU CAST INTO THE SEA; AND
SHALL NOT DOUBT IN HIS HEART, BUT SHALL BELIEVE
THAT THOSE THINGS THAT HE SAITH SHALL COME TO
PASS; HE SHALL HAVE WHATSOEVER HE SAITH."

Jesus is saying here and to you, that you can have whatsoever you saith. Whatsoever YOU saith. What are you saying? Are you saying what the Word says about you or are
you saying what you've been taught to say?

You should be confessing and believing that Jesus is working on your situation to bring you out of that prison, or sickness, or whatever the problem is, because He said so. He
said you can have what you say. If you need healing, He has
already said that by His stripes, you were healed. (1 Peter 2:
24) God didn't put that sickness or disease on you, the devil
did. (John 10:10) Before you came down with that sickness
or disease, you were in health. (III John 2) Satan has attacked
your body trying to steal your health. (John 10:10) You need
to remind him of what I Peter 2:24 says and command him
to get out of your body. After this, then stand your ground
until your total healing manifests. (Ephesians 6:10-18) The
same is true for your physical deliverance from prison. Jesus came to set the captives free. (Luke 4:18, Psalm 142:7,
Psalm 146:7)

One of the reasons why it's so hard for those incarcerated
to believe God for their deliverance is that they've been
taught an untruth. Many in prison have been taught that
Jesus put them in prison, because they were so hard-headed
on the outs. Wrong teaching.

Jesus has never put a man or woman in prison. In order
for a person to go to prison, they have to have committed
a crime. A crime is an evil act upon society. In order for
Jesus to be responsible for putting you in prison, He would
first have to have you commit a crime. If this is true, then
the Word lied because James 1:13 says, "LET NO MAN SAY
WHEN HE IS TEMPTED, I AM TEMPTED OF GOD: FOR GOD

CANNOT BE TEMPTED WITH EVIL, NEITHER TEMPTETH HE ANY MAN."

James 1:14-15 goes on to tell us that it is sin that brings us to prison. The source of all sin is the devil. We've been blaming the wrong person.

If you have asked Jesus into your heart as your personal Lord and Savior, and you're doing all you can to walk in His Word, He can set you free, if you act on the Word He has given you to make you free. I'm not talking about a brother that praises the Lord in church and then smokes dope in the cell or reads pornography and engages in homosexual acts. I'm talking about a Believer that walks in the commandments of the Lord, and I know thousands of you in the prisons across this land that are doing that.

You say, that's fine and dandy but how do I get this thing done? What do I do? Praise the Lord! I'm glad you asked that question. First off, you will never become free until you become free in your mind. (Romans 12:1-3) You must know that you are not the same person after you have accepted Jesus into your heart. You are really, truly a NEW person in Christ. Old things have passed away. (I Corinthians 5: 17-21)

I know many Christians will try to argue the point but how can we twist God's Word? Jesus didn't say that you are a new person in Christ, if you are not in prison. "Whoever" and "whenever" applies to all that are in prison, as well as to those that are not. God does not have one Gospel message for those of us that are free, and another message for those that are incarcerated.

Now remember, we are talking about God setting you free and not man. How God does it is His business. Our job is to take Him at His Word and believe Him for deliverance, not the lawyer, even though He might use the lawyer, not the prosecutor, even though He might use the prosecutor. I've had people in the past write me after I've ministered along these lines in prison and feel like I'm the one to talk with their judge, attorney, etc. Wrong. I'm not involved legally.

There are some that are. Everyone must abide in their own calling, and my calling is to preach and to teach and help with aftercare once you are released. But I've found that if I can get the truth of God's Word into you. He'll do the rest.

I began to walk around that prison and say what the Word said. I would share with any that asked about the hope I had. I'd say, "Ain't no way, I'm going to do these four years." That was my confession. And I didn't. The Word works, but we have to work the Word. The Word of God is the Sword of the Spirit

STAYING OUT

After Jesus works that miracle for you and brings you out of prison, you still cannot become lax. Satan is still your enemy and he is a relentless foe. We must be just as relentless in the things of God as he is. Just as you must stay in the Word to get your miracle, you must be just as diligent maintaining it. It might seem hard at first, but believe me, it's the easiest thing you'll ever do because the Lord is on your side.

I've seen many men come out of prison praising God, only to go back because of some very simple instructions they failed to abide by. Hebrews 10:25 says, **"NOT FORSAKING THE ASSEMBLING OF OURSELVES TOGETHER AS THE MANNER OF SOME IS."**

This is the key to staying out. You MUST find you a good Bible believing, faith believing church to attend immediately upon your release. If you do not, you are in violation of God's Word and He cannot protect you from the snares of the devil, if you are "out of place."

This seems simple, but it is not. For one thing, all churches do not know how to receive ex-offenders, and all churches do not want ex-offenders in their attendance. The other side of the coin is that many ex-offenders do not know how to receive the church. A bridge has to be built to weather this storm. An aftercare facility, an ex-offenders meeting on the outside, will provide some understanding in this area. I personally feel that every church, or ministry should have some type of an aftercare system in place to help a person coming from prison to make that successful transition. After all, the average person getting out of prison has been gone at least four years, and things can change very drastically in four years. However, the Christian volunteer coming into your facility is your best contact person.

Most volunteers coming in to do Prison Ministry are not being compensated for their efforts. So you can just believe that, if a group is faithful in coming in, they are not coming in for the pay, because there is none. The only other reason for their faithfulness is because they love Jesus, and they have to love the people that they are ministering to.

If they are a Christian group, you can just believe that they attend a church, and that church is aware of what they are doing. That volunteer can direct you to a good church upon your release that will be able to minister to your needs and more than likely, they would love the opportunity.

One of our biggest problems as ex-offenders is that we don't want to bother anyone. We're so used to getting it ourselves, that even upon our release with Jesus and a knowledge of His Word, Satan still works on our pride and has us thinking we can make it on our own. If we could make it on our own, God would never have told us to seek fellowship. We have to drop our pride, and let folks know we are going to need some help upon our release. If you do this along with your regular system of daily Bible reading and daily prayer, you will never come back as a prisoner.

ESTABLISHING YOUR MINISTRY

After you've done all of the above, then you're ready to begin praying about establishing a Prison Ministry if you feel as though God has called you to establish your own Prison Ministry. Just because you are called to be a Prison Evangelist doesn't always mean for you to start your own ministry.

God might be calling you to work with other ministries. Before you do anything, you must have a clear direction of which way the Lord wants you to go.

The first step after all of the above is forming a "Board of Directors." These are five people that will help you in forming your bylaws, etc. In order to be incorporated with the Federal government, and become a 501 C(3) Not-for-Profit organization, you need a Board of Directors. Without a board, there is no incorporation.

Contact local Chaplains in the jail and prisons and ask them how you can be of help to them. Start a Pen Pal program, through working with other Prison Ministries. God will give you the emphasis of your ministry, as you continue to seek His face.

I left prison in 1978 with a clear call from Jesus, to go out and build Him a Prison Ministry. I joined a local church, met and married my wife Juanita, and was a faithful member of my local church for three years while my ministry was being formed. I was led to begin a "Prison Ministry Church."

AFTERCARE / REENTRY

Finally, and most importantly, we need more aftercare facilities. Most prisoners are doomed for failure upon their release. After serving their time, they are released with nothing, (in most cases), but a bus ticket back to where they committed their crime. There need to be places where these persons can be paroled to, or find assistance to get started right, upon their release. Again, this will call for much prayer.

There is no set way to have an aftercare ministry, however, there are some basic principles you must adhere to, or you will have problems.

1. You must have a Resident Director (You must have someone living at the facility, at all times, to make sure your rules are being complied with.)

2. You must have some rules! (No cursing, women, men, etc.)

(For more information on starting a Reentry facility, send for my mini-book "Jesus House")

THE COST

We have an aftercare facility that we call "Jesus House." As of this writing, it is a 50 bed former nursing facility and we are located in the city of Indianapolis. Christian prisoners can be paroled to our facility upon their release from anywhere in the country. You cannot come out and spend time in the street and then apply for the Jesus House. If we did that, we would be a mission. We are not a mission. Jesus House is a "Reentry Program" for Christians leaving prison who want to continue serving God and need practical assistance.

When I'm contacted by a prisoner, I will then send them an application, and a rule sheet of the Jesus House. Based upon the return of their application and approval, I will notify the offender by letter that he has been accepted. Jesus House is a Christian facility and has rules to that effect.

Someone might be asking, "Where do I get the house?

Where do I get the money?" My answer, "anywhere the Lord leads." My prayers for a house of our own were answered by a group of local Pastors, especially Ken Sullivan of Charity Christian Center.

This group founded by Pastor Bryan Hudson, was named the Indianapolis Pastors' Gathering. The sole purpose was to pray for our city. God spoke to Ken Sullivan and he shared it with the other Pastors about purchasing us a "Jesus House." The other Pastors joined in with their prayers and finances and bought the facility for Jesus Inside Prison Ministry (JIPM) and helped with the money to remodel it.

We have recently moved into our new permanent home. A former 46 bed nursing facility.

Finally, in talking with people across the country about an aftercare facility, I'm always asked about the zoning. My answer to them is to find a place in an area that's already zoned. Someone will say, but that will be in a bad neighborhood. Right! We are to be a light in darkness.

A PERSONAL MESSAGE TO THE BLACK MAN AND WOMAN

In Genesis 1:26 God said, **"LET US MAKE MAN IN OUR IMAGE, AFTER OUR LIKENESS: AND LET THEM (MANKIND) HAVE DOMINION (RULE, AUTHORITY) OVER THE FISH OF THE SEA, AND OVER THAT FOWL OF THE AIR, AND OVER THE CATTLE, AND OVER ALL THE EARTH."**

God has made you for greatness, but it is only realized when you know who you are. "When you accept what God has said about you through His Word, you began to take on His nature."

Don't let the lies of the devil hinder you any longer. Ask Jesus to come into your heart today and reveal Himself to you. He is there right now to help and deliver you. He's waiting on you. Yes, we as Black people have a great heritage and it's in Jesus the Anointed.

Shake off those old dead religions and altitudes. This is a new day. This is the day of independence. Refuse to listen to half truths but instead embrace the only truth. His name is Jesus.

EMMANUEL McCALL writes in the 1991 edition of the HULMAN BIBLE DICTIONARY:

"The 1960's and 70's birthed another interest of Black people in relation to the Bible. The quest for Black history and Black pride led to in-depth studies of Bible personalities believed to be Black or with African identification. This has resulted in some deeper affinities for the Bible since Black people now know they are positively represented. Pride is expressed in the rescue of the   prophet JEREMIAH by EBEDMELECH, an Ethiopian (Jer.38:7; 39:15-18). SIMON of Cyrene, identified as an African, was considered heroic for helping Jesus carry the cross (Mark 15:21). Black people felt included in the embryonic spread of Christianity when seeing that representatives from African countries were among those upon whom the Holy Ghost fell at Pentecost. (Acts 2:5-11,39). Historical notions were rethought when it was discovered that Christianity did not originally come to Africa through western missionaries, but more likely from the dispersion after Pentecost, the influence of the powerful government official whom Philip baptized (Acts 8:26-37), and from the early church fathers. Recent research has determined that nine of the eighteen church fathers were African. (Clement, Origen, Tertullian, Cyprian, Dionysius, Athanasius, Didymus, Augustine and Cyril). These were men who guided the formation, crystallization, and propagation of Christian thought during the first to the third centuries A.D."

NIGER - Latin nickname meaning, "black." Surname of Simeon (KJV, Symeon) one of the Teacher-Prophets of the early church at Antioch. BLACKS were a common sight among the populations of Egypt and North Africa in the Hellenistic period. Simeon's Latin nickname suggests that he originated from the Roman province of Africa, to the west of Cyrenica. His inclusion in Acts 13:1 demonstrates the multiracial and multinational leadership of the church at Antioch.

In this same passage it speaks of LUCIUS of Cyrene. Many scholars have incorrectly identified him as a Jew from this area, however they are incorrect and study now proves that he was an African. As indicated from these scriptural truths Christianity was a dominant factor in not only the lives of Jews and Europeans, but also in the lives of Africans.

If a person was to study History from an objective view, he would find that major trouble began for the African as it did with other nations. As the world expanded so did corruption and greed.

Islam invaded Africa from the eighth century until the present with violence. So did communism in this century. Nations in Africa that are struggling and starving were plundered by communistic governments and wars. When communism failed, so did every country that had embraced it. China will fall soon.

Today Africa has found her Christian roots that began in the Bible some 1600 years before America was ever discovered. As a result, hundreds of thousands of Africans are now committed Christians and the greatest revival on Earth is going on in Africa right now and in so-called third world countries.

Don't believe the lies of the Devil any longer. I Timothy 4:1 says, **"NOW THE SPIRIT SPEAKETH EXPRESSLY, THAT IN THE LATTER TIMES SOME SHALL DEPART FROM THE FAITH, GIVING HEED TO SEDUCING SPIRITS, AND DOCTRINES (teachings) OF DEVILS."**

The devil has been spreading lies throughout history trying to stop the word from coming to pass. There are countless of religions in the earth today but none giving life. These are doctrines of the devils. They are tools of the devil to prevent you from becoming all God meant for your to be.

In Revelations 5:10 God said in His Word, **"AND HAST (past tense) MADE US (you and I) UNTO OUR GOD KINGS AND PRIESTS: AND WE SHALL REIGN (rule, dominate) ON THE EARTH."**

REFLECTIONS

People might not understand this, but I know it to be a fact, because I'm Black or African American. Actually, I'm a Christian in a Black body, and being in this body and in this present country, I had many questions concerning Christianity before my experience with Christ and afterwards. Being involved in Prison Ministry, as an inner city Pastor, I find those same questions present in the minds of my fellow brethren. Therefore, I feel a duty to share my findings on the matter praying that the Holy Spirit uses these words to free others as He has freed me.

Before I became a Christian, I was off into Islam (or a form of Islam) and various other things I was taught before I even became or professed to be a Muslim, things that kept me away from the Bible. I was taught that the Bible was the tool of the white man to enslave Blacks; that it was the 'White man's lie" I was taught that the Bible had nothing to say about the Black man by some and others said that the Bible was about Black people and had nothing to say about a white man. A person can easily become torn between the two, confused, and just forget the whole thing concerning a God. I became that person. I didn't want to hear anything about God. I had my own opinion as I believed everyone else did.

In 1978, while an inmate at the Marion County Jail on a charge of burglary, I was invited by fellow inmates to their Bible study. I attended, just to straighten out their understanding of what they believed to be the Word of God. I was prepared to share with them that the Bible was the white man's lie and was produced only to make slaves accept their position in life as coming from God. As I shared with them, I saw that I had their attention. I shared with them all that I had learned about our being taken from our homeland and that upon arriving in America, the Bible was introduced to cause us to accept our lot in life.

Blacks were told in the days of slavery and even today that a curse was put upon us because of Ham, Noah's son. However attentive these men were, they knew that they had a personal relationship with Jesus. This assurance that they demonstrated finally won me over and even though I still didn't have any answers, I desperately wanted what they had. I wanted the peace of mind they had and so I invited Jesus into my life. Upon doing that, I knew that He was real, but I still had those questions and began to dig into the Bible searching for answers and praise God, I found them. The curse of Ham some say is the reason Blacks were slaves. The curse was that God cursed Ham and placed servitude on his decendants, all Black people. However, as I searched the Scriptures, I found that God never did curse Ham. He cursed his son, Canaan.

God created Adam and Eve, and no one knows what color they were. I do know that I found that God never did curse Ham. He cursed his son, Canaan. God created Adam and Eve, and no one knows what color they were. We do know that God is not a respecter of persons. Eve may have been black and Adam white. This is just as feasible as them being White, Jewish, or any other color of the rainbow. The Bible gives no distinction as to their color. We do know however, that from these two, came blacks, whites, and all the races of the earth. Some like to say that blacks or African Americans were originally white, but because of long periods of exposure to the sun their skin was darkened. We are dealing with Genesis 9:22 where it states that Noah had three sons; Shem, Ham and Japheth.

Ham was Noah's black son, but this was before they went into the desert. They did not journey into the desert until the book of Exodus. How then did Ham become black? By using a little logic, we could suppose that when Cain slew his brother Abel, the curse or mark that God put upon him was that he changed the color of his skin. As God's judgment, he put a mark upon Cain so that everyone would know that he was different.

Could it be possible that the mark was that Cain was made black? If this were true, it would explain the appearance of Ham in Noah's family. Then again, it did not necessarily have to be Cain. Somehow or another, babies were born to Adam and Eve and they populated the entire earth until the time of the flood. The Bible tells me that Noah and his three sons, Shem, Ham and Japheth and their wives were the only eight souls left on planet earth. One of these was black, one a Hebrew and one a Philistine or White person according to Genesis chapter 10.

Matthew chapter 1 is the book of the genealogy of Jesus Christ the son of David, the son of Abraham. (Genesis 10: 21-32 says, "UNTO SHEM ALSO, THE FATHER OF ALL THE CHILDREN OF EBER, THE BROTHER OF JAPHETH THE ELDER, EVEN TO HIM WERE CHILDREN BORN. / THE CHILDREN OF SHEM; ELAM, AND ASSHUR, AND ARPHAXAD, AND LUD, AND ARAM. / AND THE CHILDREN OF ARAM; UZ, AND HUL, AND GETHER, AND MASH. / AND ARPHAXAD BEGAT SALAH; AND SALAH BEGAT EBER. / AND UNTO EBER WERE BORN TWO SONS: THE NAME OF ONE WAS PELEG; FOR IN HIS DAYS WAS THE EARTH DIVIDED; AND HIS BROTHER'S NAME WAS JOKTAN. / AND JOKTAN BEGAT ALMODAD, AND SHELEPH, AND HAZARMAVETH, AND JERAH, / AND HADORAM, AND UZAL,

AND DIKLA / AND OBAL, AND ABIMAEL, AND SHEBA, / AND OPHIR, AND HAVILAH, AND JOBAB: ALL THESE WERE THE SONS OF JOKTAN. / AND THEIR DWELLING WAS FROM MESHA, AS THOU GOEST UNTO SEPHAR A MOUNT OF THE EAST / THESE ARE THE SONS OF SHEM, AFTER THEIR FAMILIES, AFTER THEIR TONGUES, IN THEIR LANDS, AFTER THEIR NATIONS. / THESE ARE THE FAMILIES OF THE SONS OF NOAH, AFTER THEIR GENER-ATIONS, IN THEIR NATIONS: AND BY THESE WERE THE NATIONS DIVIDED IN THE EARTH AFTER THE FLOOD."

Genesis 11:10 begins: "THESE ARE THE GENERATIONS OF SHEM: SHEM WAS AN 100 YEARS OLD AND BEGAT ARPHAXAD TWO YEARS AFTER THE FLOOD; AND SHEM LIVED AFTER HE BEGAT ARPHAXAD FIVE HUNDRED YEARS, AND BEGAT SONS AND DAUGHTERS."

So we see how the world was populated. You live five hundred years and have babies every year, and then your children have kids every year. That's five generations of kids, and you'll have thousands of descendants.

In Genesis 11:12-16 we read, "AND IT CAME TO PASS, WHEN HE WAS COME NEAR TO ENTER INTO EGYPT, THAT HE SAID UNTO SARAI HIS WIFE, BEHOLD NOW, I KNOW THAT THOU ART A FAIR WOMAN TO LOOK UPON: / THEREFORE IT SHALL COME TO PASS, WHEN THE EGYP-TIANS SHALL SEE THEE, THAT THEY SHALL SAY, THIS IS HIS WIFE: AND THEY WILL KILL ME, BUT THEY WILL SAVE THEE ALIVE. / SAY, I PRAY THEE, THOU ART MY SISTER: THAT IT MAY BE WELL WITH ME FOR THY SAKE; AND MY SOUL SHALL LIVE BECAUSE OF THEE. / AND IT CAME TO PASS, THAT, WHEN ABRAM WAS COME INTO EGYPT, THE EGYPTIANS BEHELD THE WOMAN THAT SHE WAS VERY FAIR. / THE PRINCES ALSO OF PHARAOH SAW HER, AND COMMENDED HER BEFORE PHARAOH: AND THE WOM-AN WAS TAKEN INTO PHARAOH'S HOUSE. / AND HE ENTREATED ABRAM WELL FOR HER SAKE: AND HE HAD SHEEP, AND OXEN, AND HE ASSES, AND MENSERVANTS, AND MAIDSERVANTS, AND SHE ASSES, AND CAMELS."

Jesus traced his genealogy back to whom? Abraham. This is the same Abraham. Abraham goes back to Shem, which means Shem had to be Jewish because Jesus was/is a Jew. The Bible states: **"HE CAME UNTO HIS OWN AND HIS OWN RECEIVED HIM NOT."** Jesus Christ was Jewish!

The next step for Bible scholars is to take Noah's next son Japheth and trace his bloodline. When you do this, you will find interracial marriages all down through history. Take Ham's life and it starts off as Ethiopian. But Ham's bloodline like Japheth's begins to mix with other races. There is no pure bloodline in the Bible.

So really, the white man does not have a pure bloodline. The black man does not have a pure bloodline. Mexicans do not have a pure bloodline and no other race does have a pure bloodline, nor does any other race of people. So blacks came on the scene the same as everyone else. We can trace it back to Noah. God was working miracles! As we seen before, Noah had three sons. One was White, one Black, one Jewish or Hebrew. Now I've just made a few observations. These are just as good as what everybody else has come up with. Everyone else comes up with a pure thing. They say Ham was cursed, and that is why blacks are cursed today, but that is a lie. Genesis 9:18 states; **"AND THE SONS OF NOAH WHICH WENT FORTH OF THE ARK, WERE SHEM, HAM, AND JAPHETH: AND HAM IS THE FATHER OF CANAAN."**

Ham was black. Some of the Canaanites were black. There was a mixture of the Canaanites. There has been and is a mixture of every race on the earth. There have always been interracial marriages. Always. God has never been against interracial marriages except for where the Jews were concerned because the Messiah was coming through their race of people. God did not see the Jews as a better race of people, but He knew that marrying other races would turn the Jews from Him. No one else knew God, because he had only revealed Himself to Abraham. So there has been a mixture all through history. We know that Ham was black and that he was the father of Canaan. We can assume that Canaan was black or of black descent. Ask any Bible scholar in the world, and they will tell you that Ham means, 'black skinned one," and the idea of blacks being out in the sun came from Vine's expository where it states that Ham means 'tone that has been over exposed to heat, or blackened skin. Genesis 9:19. **'THESE ARE THE THREE SONS OF NOAH; AND OF THEM WAS THE WHOLE EARTH OVERSPREAD."**

Now this is just reasoning; if God said that his is how the whole earth was repopulated, and this is what He told Moses, we know this to be true, because God cannot lie. The first five books of the Bible are called the Pentateuch, and they are God speaking to Moses. If God said that the whole world was repopulated by these three sons, then one of them had to be Black, one White and one Jewish. The mixture comes from these three Genesis 9:20 **"THEN NOAH BEGAN TO BE AN HUSBANDMAN, AND HE PLANTED A VINEYARD: AND HE DRUNK OF THE VINE AND WAS DRUNKEN; AND HE WAS UNCOVERED WITHIN HIS TENT. AND HAM THE FATHER OF CANAAN, SAW THE NAKEDNESS OF HIS FATHER, AND TOLD HIS TWO BRETHREN WITHOUT."**

So Ham is the one that saw it or did it. Maybe he just went outside and made fun of his father's nakedness, showing disrespect. I don't see anything that implies homosexuality. Many believe that a homosexual act took place, but I don't believe that. The Bible tells us to honor our mother and father. I believe that he violated that principle and went outside and began laughing at his daddy because he was drunken and naked inside the tent, and disrespected his father. This is what I believed happened. (Genesis 8:23) **"AND SHEM AND JAPHETH TOOK A GARMENT AND LAID IT UPON BOTH THEIR SHOULDERS, AND WENT BACKWARD AND COVERED THE NAKEDNESS OF THEIR FATHER, AND THEIR FACES WERE BACKWARD**

AND COVERED THE NAKEDNESS OF THEIR FATHER. WHEN NOAH AWOKE FROM HIS WINE HE KNEW WHAT HIS YOUNGEST SON HAD DONE UNTO HIM."

So it reads done unto him. Maybe this is where people get the impression that Ham did something to his father. I believe that just the fact that he made fun of Noah was enough. So Noah said **"CURSED BE CANAAN."** Why then would he curse Canaan? Ham is the one that everyone believes Noah cursed, it says that Canaan was CURSED. Canaan was cursed not Ham! Now possibly he cursed Canaan, because he was Ham's son. **"AND HE SAID A SERVANT OF SERVANTS SHALL HE BE UNTO HIS BRETHREN."** This is where the idea that blacks are cursed comes from. Ham was cursed and he was black, so many believe that blacks are to be servants from now on. Many believe that this is why many blacks are poor and can't rise above poverty level. Unfortunately, many blacks believe this also. This is why blacks need to know the truth. The Bible states that Canaan was cursed, not Ham.

In the bottom notes of my Ryrie Study Bible published by Moody Press and recognized by many Bible scholars as one of the best Bibles ever printed, it states, "If Canaan was personally involved with his father Ham's sin we do not know. He might have seen Noah's condition first and told his father. But Ham is punished for his dishonor to his father by having a son who would bring dishonor to him."

Now this is wise. You see, Noah's son Ham brought him dishonor, so he cursed Ham's son so that he would bring him dishonor as Ham had brought Noah. The curse is not on the Hamites, but on the Canaanites, the inhabitant of Palestine who were first subjected by Joshua and led up by Solomon. The Canaanites long ago became extinct. The Canaanites as a race became extinct long ago. The curse, therefore, cannot be applied to anyone today! Saints of God need to equip themselves with this knowledge. Saints need to study this on their own. Blacks are not a cursed people and never have been. It has been a lie from the devil from day one. Preachers continue to preach a lie because they have not studied this issue out. They scratch their heads and say, "I don't know" and then get up and preach junk.

Every time I hear it preached, I know, regardless of who is preaching it, that he has not studied the Bible. Anyone can plainly see that Ham was not cursed, Canaan was cursed. At best, they were a mixed race but they are now extinct. God told Joshua and the Israelites to go into the land that flowed with milk and honey and defeat its inhabitants, which were the Canaanites. They wiped out most of them but saved some, so that later on Solomon could wipe out the rest. Well, if Blacks are a cursed race, why do they still exist? Two thirds of this world's population is black, not of the U.S., but of the world.

Someone hasn't studied his Bible. So Blacks definitely are not Canaanites, or a cursed people. But if Blacks were a cursed people, the Bible tells us in Galatians 3:13 **"THAT CHRIST HATH REDEEMED US FROM THE CURSE OF THE LAW."**

Everyone needs to be aware of this. Especially those who refuse to get saved because they view the Bible as a White man's lie, when the Bible is really speaking to mankind of all races and nations. God's Word is for every man. The Bible says that all have sinned and come short of the glory of God. There's not a race of people on the planet that has not sinned. Don't let race keep you from being saved. Acts 17:26 says, **"AND HATH MADE OF ONE BLOOD ALL NATIONS OF MEN FOR TO DWELL ON ALL THE FACE OF THE EARTH, AND HATH DETERMINED THE TIMES BEFORE APPOINTED."**

I've found that the bible is the most integrated book there is. All races have been used mightily by God in delivering His people and sharing the Gospel. God only has one race. The Human Race.

OUR PRESENT MINISTRY

In Mark 11:24 the Word of God says, **"THEREFORE I SAY UNTO YOU, WHAT THINGS SOEVER YE DESIRE, WHEN YOU PRAY, BELIEVE THAT YE RECEIVE THEM, AND YE SHALL HAVE THEM."**
As I studied the Word of God during my incarceration this Scripture, and Second Cor. 5:17, **"THEREFORE IF ANY MAN IS IN CHRIST, HE IS A NEW CREATURE,"** came alive in my spirit, and I began to believe that based upon these Scriptures God could, and would, work a miracle in my life. He did and these same Scriptures, acted upon, will do the same for you.

I now travel and speak in more than 150 prison meetings a year and witness more than a thousand prisoners come to Christ each year. I like to be involved in the spiritual growth of these prisoners, so there are several facets of our ministry to inmates.

First, a meeting is arranged with the Chaplain's office for our ministry to come in and conduct an evangelistic service to be held in the chapel or in a designated area to be used as such. I like working closely with the chaplain because he is the shepherd of the prison flock. And the success of any move of God in the prisons depends on a strong Chaplaincy department. We come in to be a blessing to the chaplain, as well at to the men.

Our ministry is geared toward the young and old so-called, hard-core group, which is the violent element in prison life. We take experienced volunteers and ex-offenders into the prison with us.

Prisons are sixty to seventy percent black. Most of the black inmates do not participate in services at the chapel because those services are generally labeled a "white man's religion" thus intimidating many from attending. Our ministry diffuses Satan's tactic. The fact that I'm an ex-offender and black is a major drawing card, and I'm eternally